A BOUNDLESS PRIVILEGE

A BOUNDLESS PRIVILEGE

By OREN ARNOLD

Oren Arnold

INTRODUCTION BY ALAN D. LEBARON

ILLUSTRATED BY ROSEMARY DETWILER

MADRONA PRESS, INC. / AUSTIN, TEXAS

ISBN 0-89052-007-0

Library of Congress Catalog Card No. 74-81628
Copyright © 1974 by Oren Arnold
All Rights Reserved

FIRST EDITION

Manufactured in the United States of America

DEDICATED

WITH LOVE TO MY NIECE

VIRGINIA

WHO HAS GUIDED THE ESTABLISHMENT
OF HENDERSON'S FIRST PUBLIC LIBRARY,
AND HAS HELPED WITH THE TOWN'S MUSEUM
CALLED HERITAGE HOUSE, AND WHO IS IN
FACT A LEADER AMONG THOSE PEOPLE CALLED
"THE SALT OF THE EARTH."

THE BIGGEST BOOK REVIEW IN HISTORY

 *AN INTRODUCTION*

On a spring day some years ago a young man called at the tiny office of the Chamber of Commerce in Henderson, Texas, then a county seat town holding about 8,000 people. The room seemed almost filled by the chamber staff—one middle-aged man weighing 240 pounds, a kindly, imperturbable fellow with a gentle voice. "What can I do for you, friend?" he asked.

The young man replied, "I represent a public relations firm in Houston. We have been hired by a big book publishing company to promote a new novel that will be issued in October. It was selected in a contest— the best manuscript among 180 entered by the nation's foremost writers. Therefore it became a first-prize-winning Literary Award Novel. Its title is *The Golden Chair*, and many local people are in it, some by their real names. The setting is right here in the Henderson Town Square."

"You don't say!" the chamber man's eyes brightened.

"Yes sir, and the author lived his boyhood and went to school here, still has many kinfolk in this area. He visits here often. His name is Oren Arnold. His father owned a farm and ranch about a mile north of town, and there the boy grew to manhood.

"Now, in October, if you could maybe help us get a little write-up in the *Henderson Daily News*, it would help publicize this fine novel. The town has no bookstore, but maybe we could ship in a dozen books for window display in one of the drugstores or somewhere. Anything to let the citizens know."

They discussed it a bit further, then the quiet-mannered chamber secretary made a decision.

"Son," said he, "I know all about the Arnolds, and I know Rusk County. So you just go back to Houston and let me handle this."

Some instinct told the public relations man to do precisely that. He was never seen in Henderson again. But on a midweek day the following October, the results of that interview were revealed.

On that occasion, every school in Rusk County had closed. The courts and the banks were closed, as were almost all the stores and other places of business. Rural and village stores had signs on them— GONE TO TOWN. A "little write-up" in the local paper? It had published a large "Special *Golden Chair* Edition" rich with photos, history, and folklore. So had the weekly *Henderson Times*.

About ten A.M. a parade started out of the public school grounds and moved slowly up North Marshall Street toward Town Square. Leading it in glittering costumes was the fifty-piece high school band. Next in line was a Cadillac convertible with the top down. On its rear seat were Oren Arnold and his publisher waving to some thirty thousand people—more than the total population of the county—lining the sidewalks.

At intervals came a dozen big floats. Each one depicted, with live characters in costume, a scene from the Literary Award Novel.

Mingled among those were ten precision drill teams from schools in towns surrounding Rusk County, beautiful girls exquisitely costumed, high-stepping and swaying and dancing to the exciting rhythm of ten bands. Dignitaries from Austin, mayors, judges, educators, Important People from as far away as Dallas and San Antonio, some of whom had flown their private planes in, now rode flower-decked cars in that parade, lifting their hats, waving, smiling, greeting the happy people on the walks. Some were on horses with silver-studded saddles. Six small girls rode beribboned Shetlands. About fifty Negro men and women followed a guitar player, clapping in cadence to their marching, smiling and singing and enjoying the Good Life.

From the sidelines, television cameras whirred, radio announcers chattered rapid descriptions into their microphones, newspaper cameras clicked. The people—the blessed people, often in rough old farm work clothes because they had nothing better, many of them black, all of them smiling in pride and pleasure—clapped their hands and called out toward that lead Cadillac—"Hello, Mr. Oren! Welcome home, suh, welcome home!"

Beside him in that car the publisher, a theoretically cynical and sophisticated New Yorker, suddenly broke into tears. "Never, never," he sobbed, "have I even dreamed of anything like this, much less seen it!"

"This is Texas," explained the author, standing proudly erect, smiling and waving back at the multitude. "These people are God's own."

By noon the Square was jammed. Most of the floats had circled wagon-train style into a compact unit in the center, around a decorated platform. Colored streamers and banners flashed their brilliance from all the stores and power poles. One store had been completely emptied and made into one of the major scenes from the novel, as of the year 1912, with a dozen costumed characters in living action. Nothing was sold there although it was stocked with turn-of-the-century merchandise. Sitting in a gilt-coated rocker—the golden chair—was elderly Jim Jones, affably playing the part of the grandfather in the novel. A sign behind him, enlarged from the flyleaf of the book, quoted Kipling: *"And those that were good shall be happy; they shall sit in a golden chair."* Here they were, those that were good; symbolizing the aspirations of the multitude.

The Mayor of Henderson led the author up platform steps to a microphone. A plaque of appreciation was presented. The crowd cheered and waved arms and shot off a few guns and some firecrackers. The author, his own emotions wavering a bit now, made a short speech of gratitude.

Then he jumped down and began greeting the spectators individually. Many dozens of them—"Sweet old granny people," he called them—pushed close to hug and kiss him and be loved in turn. "I remember your papa." "Your mama was my second cousin." "I used to buy watermelons when you peddled them from a buggy, a little old skinny grinning boy." "You wrote me a love note in fourth grade." "Remember when you got throwed off a yearlin' bull tryin' to ride him? WHAW!" Everybody laughed and talked and laughed again, a noisy flowtide of happiness and good will.

It took some doing for the county sheriff to get the author through the crowd to Mays and Harris Mercantile Store, an institution in Rusk County, one that had operated since before the author was born. A table had been set up on its front sidewalk, a chair put there, and about noon the day's hero started autographing books. Not one dozen, but one thousand, had been brought in by that shrewd Chamber of Commerce man.

To buy them, a line soon stretched nearly two blocks down the Square and around a corner. All the author did was scribble his name, fast; clerks were busy collecting the money. Even so, the movement was slow. Every buyer had to be handshook and/or hugged and kissed and remembered-when—"fine old granny people," humble people, good people, happy people, God's own.

The seventh one in line showed snow-on-coal and appeared to be at least 75 years of age. His old shirt and patched overalls were faded to gray but were cleaned and ironed. Scuffed shoes had slits for toe room. An ancient necktie, of sorts, was even visible, and above it ancient wrinkles made pleats that spread into a wide grin. The author came quickly out of his chair.

"Milk John!" he cried, as these two old he-man Texans hugged each other and patted backs. "Oh lord, John, how good it is to see you again! You used to help me and Mama milk our eight cows. You learnt me [he did not say taught] how to let the calf butt so I could strip the cream. Oh John, John! My friend, you can not *buy* this book, I give it to you. Here."

Milk John swelled in dignity. "No suh, Mist' Oren. I buys it."

Black and white stared eye-to-eye for a moment, then the author nodded. "Yes, of course," he hastily agreed. "I wasn't thinking. Let me write something in it, John, while you pay the lady over there, please. And John, we must get together and visit. Talk old times. Maybe go 'possum huntin'."

"We sho' will, suh, we sholy will." With pride he took his book and made way for those waiting. The author knew that John had never learned to read. But so what? Love is love.

At one-thirty the author's nephew, Billy Preston, president of the Henderson Federal Savings and Loan Association, brought his uncle a hamburger and a bottle of pop. That's all the lunch he had. He signed books and greeted people until exhausted, about four P.M. He was taken to the home of his sister, Mrs. E. M. (Opal) Preston, where he undressed to his underwear and flopped onto a bed. In two minutes he was dead asleep.

Twenty minutes later he was awakened by Ned Preston, his

brother-in-law. "Get dressed," Ned grinned. "The yard is crowded with Negro people. They demand to see you. Go down there and make them a speech."

Refreshed, inspirited, he went out the kitchen door and there under two huge spreading pecan trees another long round of hugging and handshaking began. He stood on a big empty lard can—the only podium available—and talked to them of the olden days, of life now and life to come, of patriotic ideals, of Christianity and brotherly love, of hospitality as it is practiced only in the southern American world. One of the ladies out there burst into song. Lifted her face to heaven and in a rich contralto delivered *Amazing Grace*, while everybody else gently nodded affirmation. They all shook hands again and streamed off homeward.

Dinner that night was a banquet downtown in the biggest hall available. All seats had been sold for two weeks. The food was Texan, therefore memorable; it included fresh turnip greens with cornbread, known to be the author's favorite. One short speech was made—his. No sentimentality here, just calm, friendly Texas talk; probably the best speech this excellent speaker ever made.

At departure, one of the diners, Miss Belle Gould, who taught Latin in the local high school, and who years before had been the author's schoolmate, said to him, *"The Golden Chain* is a very fine historical novel about our people and their lifeway. But I feel sure you could write a fact book on the same subject that would be even better. Why don't you?"

Tired now, he kissed Belle and said, "Some day maybe I will."

Standing beside him, his astounded and also weary publisher spoke. "Yes, do. Today we have enjoyed what was undoubtedly the greatest book review in history, and I am sure it will never be equaled. But do write your fact book, Arnold. Here in this region is the richest Americana of all."

Years have passed. The novel is out of print. And that publisher is no longer in business, but a vigorous new one has taken its place.

The fact book is presented in the following pages.

Alan D. Le Baron

OTHER RECENT BOOKS BY OREN ARNOLD:

Sourcebook of Family Humor

The Sacred Ninety Minutes

The Wild Centaur

Hot Irons, Heraldry of the Range

Mystery of Superstition Mountain

Man Against Winter

FOR CHILDREN:

Pieces of the Sky

Story of Cattle Ranching

Irons in the Fire

Young People's Arizona

PREFACE

It is not my purpose here to glorify any one individual or family. But for expediency, for authenticity and reader impact, I have chosen the one group of people through whom I can best dramatize the real objective—that of pointing up an attitude vital to successful living by anybody anywhere on earth.

That attitude has been the undergirding of what is called grass-roots America. It seems to have been held in especially high regard through the South, and I think it has come closest to perfection in the somewhat more individualized region named Texas. The setting is Rusk County, among the brilliant redbuds and the shy dogwood blossoms, the tall stately pines and the tall stately citizens.

The text "harks back." Even though our country is far better off than at any other period in its history, we are harassed today by accelerating social changes, by confusion in politics and industry and economics, and by alarmists who magnify such woes. Therefore, people everywhere are yearning for some kind of restoration. No, not of reverting back to old-time narrowness and inefficiencies, but to at least some of yesterday's heart-warming and timeless grandeurs. We sense that, while gaining much since 1900 or so, we also have lost much.

Wherefore, without cloying sentimentality, I have here reenacted some important facets of life under such Presidents as Teddy Roosevelt, Taft, and Wilson. The action, all of it accurate and genuine, also is quite typical of that period. Those first twenty years of this century were among the most important decades since the birth of Christ, because they saw the beginnings of that accelerated rate of change; they really had the last of what we might call the old and simple life, while ushering in the new. To have lived in such a time was, for me, a boundless privilege.

In presenting them I have taken minimal liberties. A few names have been changed, but only where real ones might embarrass persons still living. Where memory of the exact words used in dialogue was no longer certain, I have studiously written them "in character," as they must inevitably have been spoken. This technique, so effective in fiction, strangely offends a lot of academicians when it appears in fact writing. Those erudite folk insist that dialogue may be used only when taken from written records. But such a rule is preposterous—as witness the Holy Bible itself; it is built largely on the memory-quoted words of God and his Son.

Dozens of dedicated folk have helped me check the accuracy of details in folk speech and customs and in characterizations of the people herein. I am grateful to all of them. Very special thanks must go to my niece Virginia, who was there, and to her stalwart Texan husband, J. W. Gandy. Also to another beloved niece, Eugenia Preston Pipsaire; to my all-Texan nephew W. A. "Billy" Preston; to Miss Bessie A. Bell of Hudson, Wisconsin, for helpful critical readings; and surely to the tolerant light-of-my-life, Adele.

Oren Arnold

CONTENTS

Life is a boundless privilege, and when you pay for your ticket, and get into the car, you have no guess what good company you shall find there.

RALPH WALDO EMERSON
"Considerations by the Way"

A BOUNDLESS PRIVILEGE

 *Hospitality House*

So far as his children ever learned, no ceremony or planned policy of any kind ever entered Mr. Will's thoughts; it would have been out of character. Therefore, some latent inner force or impulse must have guided him on that occasion in 1903.

Labor on the new home had been continuous for weeks with family and friends as carpenters, amateurs all. Old Man Dobbins had installed the window rollers and cords, the door hinges and locks. Finally the day came when Mr. Dobbins put down his screwdriver and walked to five men standing there in the new front yard.

"Everything is finished, Will," said he, handing my father a heavy front-door key about five inches long.

Papa stared at it a long moment, then walked a few steps toward the fence and threw the key far out into the new patch of sweet potato vines.

He said nothing. Mr. Dobbins said nothing and, while they may have smiled gently, none of the men showed any special surprise. Perhaps their psyches and Will's were aligned. It is unlikely that any of them thought of Will's action as establishing a policy for the family future, or had any recognizable philosophy about the matter. The very word "philosophy" could hardly have been in my father's vocabulary. In all his life he had attended school only five weeks. Even that was in a backwoods log shack where his desk was shared with eight other lads. They sat on half an oak log, sawed lengthwise, with wooden legs stuck into it. The other half of the log, with longer legs, served as a table.

But from my viewpoint here in the 1970's, I can see a great significance in the incident. It wasn't merely that no home in small East Texas towns really needed a key in those distant, trustful years. A spiritual depth was involved. Kindness, in the form of hospitality, was simply instinctive. Which is the way all kindness was meant to be.

It must also have been an important occasion for Mama. She may never have seen the key, because she was "retiring," as was right and proper for wives in that pre-lib era; she would not have pushed forward into the doings of men. Not that she was meek, or fearful, or uncooperative. She was simply Woman. Wife. Mother. She had her own sphere of activity and influence, and it was wonderful. She may have heard about the key throwing, and approved. If Will wanted to act a little kittenish, let him.

Her excitement, her inner reaction, was based on the fact that she and Will at long last had gotten their children out of the figurative and literal wilderness. By dint of persistent hard work for several years, they no longer lived in a drafty three-room log house twelve miles from the nearest railroad. They now had a tight ten-room house of planed and painted lumber and artistic scrollwork in Town, just two hundred yards up a hill from the railroad itself.

True, she could not yet read or write. But four of her five children could, and I, the youngest, would soon learn. We were the five who had survived. Little stones for three more were in the pretty Maple Grove Cemetery, back down near the old place in a village called Minden.

Now she and her brood were in a fresh, clean, new environment. It amounted to entering High Society. The new farm, the new life, was in the county seat, Henderson, a magnificent metropolis. It had almost eighteen hundred people, and an awesome red-brick courthouse that dominated Town Square. I recall the clock high on the tower, the great doors under arches that looked like judicial eyebrows raised to condemn us miscreants, and the cathedral-like hush of the big courtroom with two inches of sawdust on its floor in deference to tobacco chewers. I also recall the several rugged old sycamore trees surrounding the building. In their shade, small boys could play marbles; or better yet, just sit hugging knees and fanning flies while Confederate veterans told lusty stories of The War. From their reports, I never could quite understand how the damnyankees licked us.

Violence came closer to home one dawn, when the town awoke to find the bodies of six outlaws hanging from those sycamore limbs. Under moonlight there had been a swift if illegal meting of justice—a technique I do not condone, but which conceivably might help restore sanity to America in the 1970's.

At this moment in my life, though, I was most exhilarated by the train that chugged, hissed, and rumbled majestically past our front lawn four times a day, connecting us with a main-line road sixteen miles away, at Overton. A home thus facing the railroad gave us status, prestige comparable to living now on any city's Country Club Drive. The engineer nearly always toot-tooted his whistle for me, and waved. How marvelous! We Arnolds had come a long way. Though I am sure none of us phrased it as such, it was as if we had moved from savagery to civilization.

By the time I was eight or so, the hospitality policy must have been well established. One early and very typical occasion remains etched vividly on my brain. This was in late August. The crops had all been "laid by," hence there was a blessed lull in field work because another week or two must pass before cotton would be ripe for picking and corn dried enough on the stalk to harvest. Thus, before sundown, we were all sitting on the broad south porch, when up to the side-yard gate rolled a wagon. It held a man and a woman on its seat and heaven knew how many children sardined in behind them. Mama waited, her rocker stilled. Papa waited. We all waited, staring. Mules pulling the wagon stopped, panting and lathered from humid heat. Papa stood up.

"Howdy!" he called, heartiness in his tone, his moustache spreading.

The man holding the reins nodded, then asked, "You Will Arnold?"

"Reckon so." Papa started down the eight steps.

"Well, Jim Holleman down in Pinehill said you'd put us up for the night."

"Yes." Papa ambled toward the gate. "Light. Come on in. You folks look tuckered." He turned to my older brother Grady. "Son."

Grady understood. He got up and I went with him, a barefoot tag-along. Grady would take care of the strangers' mules. My interest, a grinning one, was more in the strangers themselves. Company meant fun; a break in the endless monotony of labor on the farm, the soul killing day-in-day-out routine. Even though we now lived barely a mile from the courthouse and its sophisticated environs, we could not go there every week; we had abundant duties at home. Therefore, guests, even strangers, were doubly welcome.

There were nine ill-clad, unprepossessing, shy but defiant children. They began with fifteen-year-old Stonewall Jackson Deason, who in 1970 would have been tagged a hippie. His mop of charcoal ringlets was singularly handsome, and all but concealed his neck and colossal ears, though we made no mention of that; we well knew that a haircut cost a whole quarter, hence one a year would have been his allotment. Slender yet strong-looking legs hung from faded overalls, and ended in dirty bare feet. He wore no shirt; the day was hot. In turn were assorted other wilderness creatures, ending finally in three-year-old Admiral Dewey Deason, who was somewhat better cleaned and clad.

All were critically ill at ease in the presence of such grandeur as our big two-story house which—marvel of marvels—was actually painted, and in an impressive white at that. But they showed no hint of inferiority feeling; they glared. I was a little scared of them; I well knew how bigger boys from the country could fight "sissy" boys who lived in the big city. I therefore remained diplomatic, which is to say, I kept apart and kept my mouth shut.

But Papa, Mama, and the Deason parents got along very well. There was a formality; a spate of handshaking, of tactful inquiry about health, of comment on the weather. Presently Papa said, "I expect you folks must be thirsty. Just step over here to the well."

He drawed—he would not have used the word drew—up a rather large and heavy oaken bucket, dripping with cool invitation. Carefully he sat it on the boarded well top, then reached for a dipper. "Missus Deason, ma'am," he offered the first brimming dipperful.

It took maybe ten minutes to slake everybody's thirst, and the water was pure. Nobody who has never been truly thirsty, or who has never had a dipperful of cool water from a well twenty feet in the ground, can really appreciate the sheer luxury of such a thing. Forget your refrigerated fountains, your iced teas, your frosty mugs of beer, surely forget the inane pap called "Coke" and such. The well, the delicious water from the bosom of mother earth herself, ranks first. It has been so for countless centuries and doubtless will be so forever. Gratitude shone on the faces of the Deasons.

Our well was surrounded by an extension of the wide porch, all under roof. Small children could romp from the front door all the way around the west and south sides of the house and past the dining room, circle the well, then go on past the back kitchen door on the east, chasing or being chased by puppies and kittens. My very small Shetland pony developed a penchant for climbing the four side steps and galloping with us around that porch, much as old Rags the dog did; but Mama ruled the pony off when he started romping there alone after midnight·and breaking her geranium pots. What finally broke her tolerance was his nuzzling that water bucket and knocking the dipper into the well. I tried explaining to Mama that he was simply thirsty, and wasn't it smart of him to try to get a drink. No go. Out to the barn lot was banished mischievous Gypsy the Shetland.

But to have the family well, in effect, right inside the house itself and under the porch roof was revolutionary, as the guest Deasons well knew. Farm wells in that era were off yonder twenty, maybe thirty yards. Toting water that far to kitchen and wash shelf was simply an added burden. But then, in those years too much luxury was tacitly held to be sinful, no matter what form it took. Papa's view was not typical; his conscience had a somewhat broader horizon.

With *our* well, gangly young Stonewall Deason discovered something even more marvelous. Just swing that dripping bucket half a turn to your rear and empty it into a big flat trough waist high against a wall. The trough, painted light blue, already held four huge watermelons cooling in the well water there. One was a thin-skinned Georgia Rattlesnake, nearly three feet long and rich with goodness, possibly the sweetest of all the melon species. But under the trough Stonewall saw a one-inch metal pipe extending from it, then angling ninety degrees through that wall. "How come that there?" he demanded.

I wanted to answer him. I could have ridiculed his ignorance, in-flating my own ego; built myself up immensely. But Papa graciously spoke first, with no hint of condescension.

The thing really was a marvel. Fill the trough and—lo, a body could enter a door at the left, go down seven steps, shuck off his clothes, stand in a huge rectangular wooden tub, reach up and turn on a faucet, and have that cold well water pour onto you just like rain! The waste water then sucked and slurped its way through a hole in that big tub and the floor then drained to a distant spot where hogs drank it and wallowed in it.

The Deasons were astounded. This was truly an age of wonders, Missus Deason allowed. Papa said he didn't know about that, but I suspect he was at least an opportunist as well as a hospitable host. He suggested that the children all might just as well *try* that shower-bath thing, if they were a mind to.

If he had offered them a deed to the farm itself they couldn't have been more eager or excited. Truth is, every member of the family critically needed a bath, and no doubt wanted one. So the ritual took more than an hour, with much talking and giggling and even whoop-ing and hollering from the kids, followed by quieter but equally happy bathing by the parents. It was an occasion to remember. We must have pulled up a hundred or more buckets of well water that sundown. But the supply was inexhaustible.

Cleaned up, refreshed, the social ice broken, our guests now obvi-ously needed feeding. I well recall what mountainous amounts of "vittles" they consumed. Very probably they had not eaten much for several days. But our smokehouse still held cured hams from last sea-son, though a trifle rank here in August. Crib corn, too, had kept up our supply of hominy and meal, the hominy made right there in the back yard with lye from washpot ashes. Every other Saturday morning I had to shuck and shell half a flour sack of the flinty grains, drape the tied sack over the bare back of a bridled mare, leap up behind it, and thus ride half a mile to the stone mill. Mr. Lacey would grind my meal, josh me and poke me in the ribs, keep a little of the meal for "toll," give me a stick of lickrish—we called it that—and send me back home happy and rich with peace of mind. Therefore, cornbread with plenty of butter, speckled peas, some chewy syrup cakes, and abundant cold buttermilk, made bountiful nourishment.

During the meal there was one regrettable incident. That day I had caught two harmless green lizards about six inches long, graceful, pretty things. I had them in some grass in a box under the house, where my dog Rags sniffed and rumbled at them. Sensing now that the Deasons were getting too much attention, I contrived some for myself. Those pet lizards were accommodating. Squeeze one's jaws a tiny bit, and its mouth would open; I could then attach it to an ear lobe. No, it would not let go, but just hang there. I do not know why; never did know. So at table this night I wore two lovely green lizards on my ears—unnoticed at first. But when Missus Deason quietly ordered her fourteen-year-old daughter Cleota Belle to "help" by pouring the buttermilk, Cleota Belle leaned across my shoulder to fill my glass— and her bare arm brushed one of my lizards.

Milk cascaded from the pitcher onto table and floor, Cleota Belle screeched, and I could not hide my lizards quickly enough to act innocent. I will not go on; the aftermath is unpleasant, even in long memory. Suffice it to say that I got more attention than I had wished for. From Mama.

It was the iciness of the buttermilk that enabled Stonewall Jackson Deason to ferret out yet another miracle of science. He was getting over his shyness, so he asked how come the buttermilk was so cold, colder'n it could have been just from a long skinny bucket lowered into the well, as was the farm custom.

Mama pointed to a huge, heavy wooden box in the corner of the dining room, then lifted the thick hinged lid for him. Stonewall looked down into that box and his eyes bugged, his mouth popped open. By gum, there was *ice* in that there box, right here in August! I be dad-burned! Doggone! Jest lookahere, Pa.

Stonewall stooped low to see the pipe that drained melted ice water through the floor and into a pan under the house, where the chickens and the dog could drink. The boy was truly excited by this city miracle. However, he suddenly realized that he had slipped out of character and broken his own image of himself, so he resumed defiant, glowering silence. I let him alone. I knew better than to nag him, as I felt tempted to do, from the heights of my city sophistication. He was nearly twice my size. From the others also there was a great hullabaloo about that icebox, just as there had been about the crude shower bath. Apparently there was no end to the modern scientific marvels in the new Will Arnold home at Henderson.

It is natural now to wonder what we did with eleven unexpected overnight guests. Wherefore, we must further envision the house.

Its architectural style was pure East Texan. Meaning that it had negligible originality and beauty, even negligible convenience, yet somehow was homey. Very probably the word "architect" was unknown to Papa and Mama shortly after the turn of the century. How foolish it would have been, how wasteful, even sinful therefore, actually to have hired some fellow to draw a picture of the house you proposed to build! If you had just come to Town from the back-country piney woods.

Later, when oldest child Tip married pretty Norma and built their house near ours, I saw how it was done. Tip took a two-foot section of newly planed pine plank twelve inches wide and, with a stub pencil, sketched out his floor plan, marking in the dimensions. This took maybe half an hour. And that was all.

About 1910, when we papered our parlor's bare plank walls, I discovered that the south wall was three inches wider than the north. But what of that? A three-inch strip had been set in to correct the discrepancy. I had to allow for it as I tacked on the cheesecloth "canvas" to which the paper would be glued, and Sis—she is my sister Opal, still hale and hearty at age eighty—had to cut a narrow strip of paper for it. The entire house was somewhat like that; out of kilter here and there; odd measurements, with many strange angles, turns and nooks, a grand place for hide-and-seek, and ghosts. But it was solid. It had joists, rafters, and cross supports twice the needed size, hence it defied even the worst windstorms.

From the wide front door with stained glass panels on each side of it (a touch of real grandeur) a wide hall ran down the middle, with two big rooms on each side. Then at the back end of it was the dining room. There the hall left-turned past the kitchen and ended in a north door to a porch, which later was walled in to make a bath.

All ceilings were eleven feet up, which meant that ninety percent of all heat from our fireplaces and wood-burning heaters rested waste-fully in the upper strata, whereas our feet were eternally cold.

Big double doors at the turn of that hallway, to the right, opened onto that wide south porch where most of the summer "living" was done. There was no formal living room. But there was "Mama's room," which was large enough for two double beds, and eight chairs before the great fireplace with the ugly Seth Thomas clock dutifully tick-tocking in stately dignity on its mantle, eternally warning us that man's time on this earth is limited, and that we should get up and get the chores done and the farm work under way. We could hear it all over the house when the hammer hits its circular whorl of steel every thirty minutes, making a *whan-ng-ng-ng* that was more commanding than melodious; unless Papa forgot the ritualistic winding every eighth day.

The Deason family was fascinated by that outspoken clock in that huge room. "Art" pictures hung framed on the walls in there. I knew they were real art, because each one cost a whole quarter, before fram-ing. One showed a might-nigh nude young woman in a filmy gown or something, fleeing from a black storm cloud behind her, and a hand-some young man running at her side holding a red cape to protect her from the elements. Just what in the high hopping hades she was doing out in a harsh wind and rain storm barefooted in the dark of night I never quite understood. But I *did* easily identify with that handsome hero trying to help her.

"That there is a maiden in distress," I explained loftily to the Dea-son kids, quoting my older brother who, I now think, was slightly cynical about it. At the time, we boys were properly awed; the picture caused us to envision ourselves as knights in shining armor, or some-thing, which is the real test of "art." Isn't it? I mean, wasn't it? To-day the criterion may be different; but not necessarily better. God help us, I have recently seen a painted picture of a cabbage head with a human eye in it, all of it melting and draining over the edge of a table. But my parents, though imaginative, were not surrealists.

Every detail of that big room is etched on my memory, even now. As a little fellow I slept in one of the double beds, Mama and Papa in the other. If Papa snored too obnoxiously—which was very likely, any night—Mama would move over with me. Why *do* some people snore? It is an abomination. Anyhow, each winter night, the family and any guests gathered in this room before the fireplace. But come eight P.M., no matter what, Papa yawned, stretched, stood up, went quietly back beside his bed in semidarkness, undressed down to his long heavy underwear, crawled between the sheets, pulled up the quilts, and promptly went to sleep. Nobody said anything, or even appeared to notice; guests least of all. Will Arnold's life was his own, and fatigue was an understood thing, and courtesy an imperative. To us kids, who sometimes dared giggle at it, Papa's snoring was the rumble of a yearling bull. The other adults stayed up late; sometimes until nine-thirty or later.

Up front, south, was the parlor.

It was, let us say, comparable to the Grand Ballroom in a modern Hilton Hotel. It held the piano, some fancy black-upholstered furniture, and an "art square" rug. Papa's cotton must have commanded a good price for a year or two around 1900 or oh-one or oh-two. Also, Mama's incubator for baby chicks was in there. Yes, in our parlor.

Seldom used socially, that parlor was the ideal quiet place for hatching 115 (I well recall the count) eggs in the hen-like warmth of a small kerosene lamp. Few chickens have entered the world amid such splendor. It was my boyhood duty to turn the eggs each morning; a hen does it with her feet. All of us took pride in the first weak "peep-peep" of the babies who had just chipped their way into the dangerous world. The Deasons beheld that incubator with a silent disbelief akin to awe. I don't much blame them.

A stereoscope also was in there. As the Deason children discovered with renewed awe, you could put two pasteboard photos of Niagara Falls on the stereo slide, and be dogged if the falls didn't come alive in three dimensions, just like for real. By now the Deasons appeared to behold us Arnolds as beings who were somewhat more than mortal; discovery is wonderful, yet a person can stand just so much.

"There's some ketch to this here," avowed Cleota Belle, the most learned of that clan, looking behind the pasteboarded pictures as if checking for actual water. I couldn't help her, I didn't understand 3-D phenomena myself. For that matter, I don't understand 2-D "pitchers" that come in such sharp detail and such perfect color into our homes today. Even as I write this, I can look left and watch a football game

better than if I had a seat on the fifty-yard line, and I well agree that
"there's some ketch to it." Who of my generation can possibly understand television? Back there, I warmed to Cleota Belle.

The Deasons had never even seen a piano before, for theirs was a
very backwoodsy clan. So when Sis played *Rock of Ages* for them,
Missus Deason cried a little; she had recently lost a child. But when
Sis banged into *Alexander's Ragtime Band*, Mr. Deason's eyes lit up
and he started swaying a little and snapping his fingers, and first thing
we knew he was belting out the words with her and smiling and having himself a high old time. It's a good thing there were no eggs
incubating at the moment; they wouldn't have hatched.

Mama did not smile at the musical hijinks; she always took a dim
view of ragtime ryhthm, and I shudder to think of her reaction if she
had to hear what today is called rock. In her teen years, Sis used that
parlor for courting, and eventually for her wedding. No funerals were
ever held there; nobody dared die in the pleasant living during the
lifetime of this white house on the hill.

The stairway to the second level was in the wide hall. My boyish
bottom acquired many a callous sliding down the banister rail. Only
three rooms were upstairs, but a small railed porch extended over the
front steps below. A body could hide on that porch and spit down on
other children unwarily climbing our front steps. But this was in-
advisable; mothers can be unreasonable about such sport.

The house faced west. For twenty years or so the sun was screened
off the lower front porch by a luxuriant Marechal Neil rose which
climbed and preened itself like a vain bird on the trellis there. It
reached far above the roof then wound through the upper porch
banisters and on up to the roof above that. I assured the Deasons
that it had ten million blossoms on it, and that didn't seem much of
an exaggeration. The gorgeous thing was one of the glories of Henderson, and Missus Deason, beholding it with hands clasped to her
breast, murmured, "My my, I just do declare!" Mama had high status
in Henderson because of that rose, as well as for other reasons, as we
shall see.

The front yard, fenced with ornamental white palings, held two
young magnolia trees, which my mother also loved. In 1973 I visited
those trees. They had become enormous. In their shade, my built-in

calendar flipped its pages backward. I had played marbles on the hard white sand under those trees, had wallowed there with my dog Rags, soothed by the strong, permeating fragrance of the blossoms high above. Sometimes we could smell them all over the home and barn-yard area, and just one, put in a dining-room vase, could be almost sickeningly sweet. It is under this tree that Southern Belles allegedly—and often, actually—get kissed and engaged to dashing Rhett Butler-type heroes; the atmosphere there is right for romance. Once at age nine I my own self kissed Bonny Flanagan there, but shucks, it didn't seem like anything to get excited about. Not then. I knew that my beautiful big sister Opal had gotten herself kissed under one of those trees by Ned Preston, and look what happened to *her*! Married him, and had a mess of kids, and now a passel—I am using localisms still in vogue at Henderson—of grandchillun, even some greats. And why not, I asked myself, bemused there in 1973? Sis was eminently kiss-able, away back there in time, and she and Ned "done well" in life. Yankee people, Nawtheners, tend to smile a trifle condescendingly about romancing under our Dixieland and Texas magnolia blossoms. Truth is, they behold us with secret envy.

That recent day, I plucked one super-fragrant blossom sixteen inches across, a thing of velvety white. And thought poignantly of Mama and of how such beauty had touched her, half a century ago.

Outside the front paling gate—its posts had round wooden balls on top, painted white too—was a hitching post. Then six rows of sycamore trees adorned the great lawn that swept like an emerald apron down the slope to the next fence, paralleling the railroad. Those trees, plus several elms closer by, made a proper setting for our white mansion. I had never seen a sycamore before, and neither had the Deasons; they "ohed and ahed" over them, stroked the slick whitish-pink bark, which was eternally peeling and littering, and added them to their mental listing of new-wonders-found.

Their bark offered ideal places on which to carve girls' initials with your own in interlocking hearts. In October huge maple-type leaves picked up the hues of sunset and held them, and we pressed one big leaf in the family Bible every year we lived there. I wonder what ever became of those leaves? Perhaps some later-day person read a bit of family life and lore, coming onto the fragile, crackly things.

In 1971 I found the world's largest sycamore tree. It is growing
in faraway Laguna Hills, California, in Aliso Park. *Aliso* is Spanish
for sycamore. This one is an unbelievable 14 feet thick at its base.
Main limbs are 6 feet in diameter. Total spread is more than 150 feet
—half a football field. This tree was 50 years old when the Pilgrim
Fathers landed in 1620. Only a few of those on our old place at
Henderson are left standing now, but they are yet in their infancy.
The main one with the carved hearts was gone, but then love is tran-
sient anyway if you are under age 15. Another special one *was* still
there in 1973. Its limbs had held my rope swing and my trapeze.

The visiting Deason family, especially the children, quietly ex-
plored all these wonders in and around our house. They knew about
the train but most had never seen one. So, when one was due in from
Overton, I proudly took the young folk down that front lawn of
sycamores to view the smoke-belching thing at close range. Thought-
fully, I brought along some ordinary pins from Mama's sewing basket. I showed my guests how to place these pins on the iron rails
in sets of two, crossed like an X. When the train rolled over them,
the immense pressure of its wheels converted those pins into forms
like tiny welded scissors—another miracle to the Deason girls, although Stonewall sneered.

But Stony was awed by the train, as all of them were. He had to
hold little Admiral Dewey, who cried in fear of the great chugging
monster even though the fireman waved genially and clang-clanged
his bell. We traipsed on back up the hill. Cleota Belle—her mama's
daughter—murmured, "I declare, it do beat all!" She meant the train,
and I knew that she spoke for the whole Deason family. Even now,
I still share her awe of any passing train. I think most people do. But
the sonorous *whonk-whon-n-nk* of a diesel can never hope to compare
with the majesty, the haunting loneliness, always inherent in the steam
locomotive's distant *whoot whoo-wooooooooooot* heard at night in the
isolation of a farm or ranch home. That sound of the choo-choo is
unforgettable for those of us who are old enough to remember it.
For an American century it spoke of grand doings far away; of allur-
ing glamor and romance—somewhere.

Many other wonderful bits of living, many memorable incidents,
took place on that long porch that curved around three sides of our

farmhouse. One I must tell. About two A.M. on a night in 1910 my father shook me awake, led me to the east porch beside the dining room and the kitchen, and there put an arm around my shoulders. Nothing was said, at first. But lo, stretching in incredible majesty across the sky from a huge rounded nose far to the north, a brilliant fantail of light splayed out far to the south and disappeared behind our hay barn!

The impact was numbing. The phenomenon dominated the entire panorama of night, with light so profound that it seemed almost audible. Frightened, I finally let my breath go again, when Papa spoke.

"Halley's Comet, son. It will come back again in the year 1985. You are just ten now. Perhaps God will let you see it again."

Perhaps He will.

Good dog Rags bayed at it. Cattle in the pastures hurried up to the cowpens, lowing. A mule screamed and kicked a fence gate down. An owl screeched, and all of Mama's chickens were cackling and squawking, and even the day birds in the trees had come alive and were stampeding around in the weird night sky. We couldn't blame any of our creatures; we ourselves weren't too sure but what the world was coming to an end. We stayed on that back porch until dawn.

Forty feet or so away on the south porch, nearest the side yard gate, a juvenile dormitory was set up that night the Deasons spent with us. Papa and Mama gave Mr. and Mrs. Deason their own bed in Mama's room—anything less would have been unseemly—and they themselves slept on a pallet in the parlor. But the Deason kids slept on quilts on that porch.

There were no pads or pillows. The term "bed roll" was not yet in the language, so far as I knew, and even blankets were unknown to us. Our covers were brilliantly colored and patterned patchwork spreads with a layer of cotton inside each, the whole hand-quilted with tiny, artistic stitches. Grandmothers, maiden aunts, widows, and sometimes mothers, if they ever found a few free hours, gathered periodically to make such things in an era before cocktail and bridge parties. They would let down a wooden frame from little rollers attached to the ceiling, sit around it and sew and gossip, and maybe dip snuff. My quilt had a huge Texas star on it. Today I wish I knew whatever became of it.

On that night I left my soft bed, silently took my star and snuck out to join the young Deasons. There'd be more fun out there, I figured. And so there was. Mrs. Deason herself had to come out and scold her brood for giggling. In the darkness, I doubt if she ever knew I was there. I had triggered the giggling by moaning like a ghost.

Sister Opal was in her room up front across the hall from the parlor. Brothers Tip and Buck were in their room upstairs, over hers. Grady slept in his room, which was the one right near us on that porch. Or tried to. He got fed up with us, though he wasn't so old himself, just then. I believe he must have been seventeen, which meant that he carried a full work load on the farm. So it was he who, rather late that night—probably eight-thirty or nine—called out his window to us on our pallets, speaking with lofty dignity. "It would be appreciated if you children would quiet down. We have to start mowing hay early tomorrow."

That settled me and the Deasons. For one thing, Grady was much bigger than I, and physical pressures could be brought to bear. So we just figured to lie quiet for a few moments until he could go to sleep, then resume our moaning and giggling. Mama woke us at dawn saying come to breakfast.

My recollection is that the Deasons stayed one night, then drifted on. They never entered my life again. But they were not unique in our family experience. Not once, or twice, but many dozens of afternoons, complete strangers came up to our side gate seeking hospitality, or late at night ventured into the yard and rapped on the porch floor. They may or may not have been sent to the Arnold home by somebody far out in the country who knew us. They may simply have heard of us and gambled on our friendliness. They were never disappointed. Nor did we ever even remotely consider their arrival an imposition. It was a normal, natural thing for them to do, we reasoned, or at least Mama and Papa did. I recall only being pleased with the company, and sometimes awed by the profusion of it. Papa's and Mama's reputation thus had spread. It was a good something.

That parental policy, I may say in passing, must have ingrained itself in all five of us Arnold children. When we grew up and established homes of our own, the same policy held. Even in the years since 1930 or so, right on into the present 1970's, my own house is "open." My Texas-born Adele, though originally a city girl, has cooked, I suppose, ten thousand extra meals for guests, expected and unexpected. And many a time we ourselves have slept on pallets or second-best beds so that company could have our best. This sometimes astonishes modern guests, but we like the policy we inherited.

When in 1942 we built our own beloved five-bedroom four-bath highly picturesque Indian pueblo home of adobe bricks at 34 West Pasadena Avenue in Phoenix, Arizona, I experienced a moment of nostalgia, a surging sense of drama.

Remembering, I took the front door key and threw it far out into a vacant lot among some wild flowers.

 *Uncle Johnny*

Today I can not recall, nor can anyone else in our family, exactly when John Barry arrived to make his home with us.

He was with us before we left Minden—an old, browned-out photograph attests to it. But surely my early mental pictures of him remain vivid. He was slender and, to a small boy, seemed treetop tall. Very probably some of his Irish genes had come into my own bloodstream, for John was my mother's full brother, and my nickname, "Skeeter," accurately tells how I looked. The total Irish of him was apparent in his red hair and red waterfall moustache, but more so in his deep sentimentality and quietly rich sense of humor. Happily, I also inherited some of that. Uncle Johnny seldom laughed big. But he often chuckled. He shook, and twinkled, and smiled in a manner that spread the moustache intriguingly. His kindliness was profound. I wish my inheritance had included all of that.

Seemingly more important at the moment, from my very juvenile point of view, was the fact that Uncle Johnny was a scholar. Wonder of wonders, he not only read the Holy Bible and taught it in Sunday school as a devout Presbyterian, but he also read other good books. They awed me by their size, their leather-bound façades, and especially their titles. Somebody's *Commentary. Biography of Robert E. Lee. Power of Will. History of the Civil War. What Every Gentleman Ought to Know. Calculus in Science.* Oh I remember clearly, because I myself was bookwormish as I progressed in grade school. I read everything that G. A. Henty and Horatio Alger ever wrote. I thumbed Uncle Johnny's library items, but they baffled me. Not even he could make me understand what "calculus" was, and nobody ever has yet, although some distinguished professors at Rice University tried! I was no Abe Lincoln, improving my mind by the light of a pine-knot fire.

Uncle Johnny had attended Rock Hill Institute, once a respected "normal" school in the rural depths of Rusk County, near our family's village of Minden. I didn't know then, nor have I ever been able to learn, what a "normal" school was, but the term was once common in America. Apparently it emphasized preparation for teaching, with perhaps some elements of modern-day junior college. It is strange that such a school should have been in that particular spot, surrounded by poverty and illiteracy; and shameful that it didn't progress and endure. To this day, Minden isn't much. It might have been; might have become a renowned center of education, what with the oil gushers that soon shot skyward nearby, and the resultant flood of money into Rusk County. The take-charge leadership was missing.

At any rate, Uncle Johnny lived with us all summer but, come September, he would take suitcase in one hand, a parcel of books in the other, and walk twelve miles to teach in a very rural school. He would bed and board out there with some farmer. We often felt that he could do much better; could teach maybe here in Town itself. But no. He said he felt called. We understood that. Preachers, the good ones, we knew, were called. A life of selfless service was respected. That alone would have made him doubly welcome in our house.

But he also added considerable social prestige, much as the railroad did, at least in the minds of my illiterate parents. I am not sure, but I have often suspected that it was Uncle Johnny who finally was able to teach Papa to write a crude sort of hand, enough to send us boys an occasional short letter in college, and to sign checks. If Uncle Johnny tried, he never did succeed in teaching Mama how to write; we never had a letter from her, and she signed any legal documents with a crossmark. Only she did not make it an X; hers was a holy cross, but just as legal when witnessed. She was not openly ashamed of her limitations there. She would often show some document to friends, pointing to her brother's beautiful Spencerian signature as witness, and mentioning his erudition ever so casually. The friends were properly impressed, and she basked in the reflected glory. Later, I did my own bragging about Uncle Johnny, mentioning that "he learnt me nearly everything I know." If he did, it couldn't have strained him much.

Papa and Mama both learned to read very well, Papa the *Dallas Morning News*, the *Henderson Weekly Times*, and the *Rusk County News*, edited by his good friend, Colonel Bob Milner, who actually became President of Texas A. and M. College and owned a farm near ours. Knowing a college president was something, I tell you! Uncle Johnny and Colonel Bob used to sit together in Courthouse Square in the shade of sycamore trees and do what they called philosophizing. I snooped on that, hanging around; but shucks, it wasn't nothing but talking, I reported to my pals Tunk Griffin and Lank Wood. But my interest in culture there paid off, even so. The philosophers would nearly always give me a nickel to take over to Cover and Rayford's Grocery Store and buy myself a cold strawberry soda in a bottle with a stiff wire loop on top. I'd bop that wire with my grubby hand and pop would spew out. Fat Mr. Cover would say, "Stop messing up the store, Oren." Like as not, though, he'd cut me off a big hunk of cheese to eat with it, free.

Uncle Johnny taught Mama to read those papers, along with *Comfort Magazine*, published, I remember, in Augusta, Maine. Then she progressed into *Woman's Home Companion, Ladies' Home Journal, Pictorial Review*, and on through *The Bible in Large Type* which Uncle Johnny gave her. In her last decade she was as learned as any woman in town, thanks largely to a scholarly brother and long winter evenings before the fireplace.

In summertime, Uncle Johnny would rest by sitting on the broad south porch and talking to anybody around. His was never Irish "blarney" or small talk. It might concern miracles in nature—the way birds build nests, or bears hibernate, or opossums have sixteen or so babies, all of which you could hold in a teaspoon; that sort of thing. No wonder Tunk Griffin and Lank Wood and I were fascinated, sitting dirty-toed and cross-legged as his disciples. At other times he would venture adult ideas and philosophies that plainly were beyond most farm mortals. But everybody listened, respectfully. Even the Negroes would nod and murmur, "Yessuh, that is co-reck."

Sometimes he just sat and thought. *Thought*, mind you. He could "think out" solutions to problems that he or Papa or Mama faced. Often he whittled. It was unwise to nag him when he was whittling, because I am sure he whittled to stimulate his thinking. Moreover, likely as not the result would be a toy windmill or a whistle or a little animal for me. But if in such moments of his concentration I or any other brash youngster dared ask him what he was making, he would say "Layoes to catch meddlers." For years I wondered what a "layo" might be. I still wonder.

The social prestige that he added to our family was enhanced by the fact that he dressed better than most of us. *His* trousers were never baggy, wrinkled, or soiled for long; he personally cleaned and ironed them. *His* shirt was seldom frayed or soiled; he personally washed and ironed every one. *His* shoes were always neatly blacked; he showed me how to mix soot from the chimney with melted suet to make a waterproofing-polish compound. It was excellent.

There was only one drawback to Uncle Johnny's personality, only one flaw in his perfection. He stank. For no reason ever apparent to us, he was mentally or psychologically allergic to bathing. Though meticulously tidy and neat and clean of hand and face—he washed before every meal—he sewed himself into long red underwear come November 1 and did not remove those stitches until the following April 1. I knew it, we all knew it; but I was not to say anything about it, mind you. Or Papa would have clouted me; or even Grady. A man of John Barry's stature deserved not snickering derision but respect.

Years later, when I was at Rice Institute (now Rice University) in Houston, a distinguished professor of biology, Dr. Edgar Altenburg, told our sophomore class that there is no clinical reason for bathing, that it really has no bearing on bodily health, that millions of human beings never bathe. At the moment, I was campus correspondent for the big daily *Houston Chronicle*, so I "wrote up" what the professor had said. The Associated Press put it on its wires, and the short piece made front pages all across America. My mind drifted back, wonderingly, to Uncle Johnny Barry, the sage of the piney woods.

He paid for his bed and board by working incredibly hard with us all summer. Nobody could plow a straighter furrow than John Barry. Nobody could load a wagon more skillfully with hay. Better yet, he was more than a novice at veterinary science. He knew what to do with a good cow that was having trouble birthing a huge bull calf, or one that had teat fever, or had been bitten by a water moccasin. Unfortunately, he had not known what to do when years before, a moccasin bit one of his own fingers. Instinct probably saved his life. He "milked" the finger while sloshing it in pond water getting out all the poison he could. But the finger healed as a small, hard, crooked bony thing, at which I used to stare in childish wonder. I never quite dared ask him about that deformity, but Papa told me.

It was Uncle Johnny who, one November when rains and hail and floods had made the farm enterprise a desperate failure, came to Papa and silently handed him five hundred dollars in golden coins. We never knew where he got them. But Uncle Johnny was miserly; never spent an unnecessary dime, except to slip me one now and then. Papa took the money and we lived on it for months; then paid it back as calmly as he had received it. I believe no words were ever spoken about the transaction, first or last. It's just the way "business" was in such circumstances; business and friendship and hospitality. And brotherly love.

When Uncle Johnny died at age ninety-two, still a bachelor, still a smiling old red-haired Irishman, he was known to have collected some fifty thousand dollars in gold. Oil had been discovered in Rusk County, and royalties on poor sandy land that he owned had paid him that much. This we know because my brother Tip became county assessor and had access to the records. But Uncle Johnny didn't trust banks. He had been with us when a thief named Wettermark absconded from a private bank in Henderson with all the funds in its safe, including six thousand dollars that belonged to Papa.

Papa and his friend Bill Shadden got their shotguns, mounted their horses, and combed the county for days, but Wettermark escaped to South America, we eventually learned. When in moments of carelessness Papa used to damn him audibly, Mama would say no, we must pray for him. I suppose *she* did. I couldn't bring myself to do it, and I doubt if Papa or Uncle Johnny did. I would sure bet that Bill Shadden didn't; he was a tough, hard, though fair-minded, man and, if he could have gotten his hands on Wettermark, justice would have been done. As for Uncle Johnny, in that era before bank deposits were insured by the federal government, he simply started burying gold coins in fruit jars. People have searched and searched for thirty years.

I like to imagine that about 1980, maybe, some good old Texas boy, bulldozing ground to build a new schoolhouse or something, will push his blade into a lot of glass and his eyes will bug out in astonishment and——.

 *Bread upon the Waters*

Uncle Johnny, being kin, was accepted by us as being permanent without anyone's ever mentioning it or appearing even to think about it. The alternative for him would have been a lonely place apart, somewhere. This way, we were all fortunate.

We were fortunate also when our two other "permanent" members arrived.

This happened, as best I can recall, in 1907, possibly 1908. The time of year and the setting were much the same as when those Deasons arrived to spend the night with us. The day was Sunday, the hour about four P.M.

At the moment, I was watering Mama's geraniums. There were possibly three dozen plants in pots setting on stairstep risers on the southwest corner of our porch. I had a bucket of clean water, fresh from the well, and a gourd dipper.

I believe I have not mentioned those geraniums before. In retrospect I realize that they, along with our climbing Marechal Neil rose, were significant. They represented a rural mother's reach for beauty in a practical milieu that had too little room for it. I used to see her hold the gorgeous blossoms to her cheeks, loving them. An Irishwoman, she must have been blest with a romantic nature, as most Irish folk are, though we did not consider such intangibles at that time.

She had simply made Papa construct those risers, then make her a pit with a cover near the porch to protect the plants from winter's sleet and cold.

On this particular Sunday afternoon I was pouring a dipper of the cold well water into each pot, on Mama's orders. My mind, however, was off somewhere in the imaginative world of boy interest, so I did not notice another wagon coming up the front lawn road. I came out of my reverie only when I heard a new voice.

"Mistuh, is yo' pappy home?"

That in itself was drama; never before had anybody called me Mister. When I turned I had to look up, even though I was on the porch two feet above the ground. He was that big. He also was very black, but with what were then called "white features," meaning that his face showed none of the thick-lipped coarseness often associated with his race.

His smile said distinctly that he liked me; that he liked all children. Children can sense that in any adult.

"Yes," I replied. I almost said "Yes *sir*," and no doubt he merited it, especially from a little squirt such as I. But that wouldn't have been meet and proper; not white-to-black, in East Texas in those years.

"My name George Austin," he informed me. "What's yours?"

"Oren."

"You Mistuh Will's boy?"

I nodded. I was at a loss. But I had to do or say something. The germ of hospitality must already have spread to me, young as I was. So I said, "You want a drink? It's clean." I held out a brimming gourd.

He gulped the cool well water, wiped his mouth on the back of his hand, and sighed his thanks. "That mighty good." He patted his belly. "Hot today."

It was July. I well knew because my birthday was coming up next Wednesday and Mama had promised me a whole dime. Not a nickel, a dime. Modern youngsters can have no conception of what that bounty meant. I have a grandson who on his seventh birthday got seven dollars, not to mention a pile of fancy gifts. I'll wager I was happier with my dime.

George stood there sizing me up. Quite likely he tagged me ac-

curately then and there, even as I had instinctively tagged him. Re-
ferring to myself a moment ago, I used the term "little squirt," and
he may have used it, too, in his mind. It was a common one in that
era, and reasonably accurate. Refined moderns in the 1970's may not
know that it referred to physiological performance. Boys of all ages
would naturally foregather now and then, in the barnyards, in woodland or field or beside a stream. It was a frequent game to see who
had the most built-up pressure. At my age I could not be in the serious competition; I could only hope for the future as I, too, grew big.
Wherefore I was in the accepted category of "little squirt." The competition was the most fun when held on fresh snow. I am told that
such games are still popular.

But George had called me Mister. Such man-to-man courtesy so
endeared him to me that I put on my best manners. I said, "Papa's
asleep on his cot on the back porch," with which I broke and ran
noisily around there.

My clatter awoke Papa. He sat up, hit me a pretended blow for
making noise, stood, and stretched.

"There's a man and a woman," said I, pointing.

He peered out through the shimmery hot air. The woman was still
in the wagon seat. The man had taken her a dipper of my cool water.
Now he walked to the higher porch steps near our well.

"Evenin', suh," the black man began. We never used the term
"afternoon" in our farm world; anything after midday was evening.
"You Mistuh Will, suh?"

How sharp the picture is! It is strange, how the mind skips and
jumps, leaving many incidents blanked out altogether, others etched
as if they had happened today. His bearing, his manner were no whit
obsequious. He had a unique, relaxed dignity. Today I realize that he
was a far cry from the typical black. Conceivably, he was "oppressed"
by circumstances or something. If so, he didn't seem to know it. I
have never encountered a more self-contained, happier individual. I
can not now conceive of his ever marching with a silly placard or
stooping to violence in protest against life. But then, that was more
than sixty years ago.

Papa answered him. "Will Arnold, yes." He walked toward the
steps. "Looking for our place?"

The Negro laughed quickly, heartily. He also winked down at me. "Coming here to work, suh."

"Work! Here?"

"Tha's right, Mistuh Will. Me and Ellen both. Yo' brother-in-law sent us. He say you and Miss Archie killin' yo'selves. Me, I'm yo' new fo'man. Ellen, she Miss Archie's cook. Dr. Dawson hisself say so."

"But hold on here! I can't——."

"Naw suh." The man laughed again. "Rest yo' mind, suh. We take care of ourselfs. We sleep in the barn tonight, find us a place maybe tomorrow. You go on back, lie down, rest. When you git up in the mawnin', Ellen, she have everybody's breakfast cooked. I have all the stock fed. And where the milk buckets, suh? I does the milkin'."

Papa was tied. Events had moved fast, and behind his back. Charlie Dawson—Charles Dawson, M.D.—who had married papa's sister Evie, was indeed an intelligent man even though he served humanity from that isolated village of Minden, where we had begun as a family. Heaven only knew how many lives he had saved, how much misery he had alleviated. Once, I recall, the Texas Medical Society, meeting in Dallas, honored him for distinguished work in treating digestive disorders. But here he had known that Will and Archie Arnold were killing themselves with overwork, because at this stage the Arnold sons were leaving the nest. Tip had gone to college in West Texas. Buck was off to Austin to study law at The University of Texas. Soon Grady would be going to medical college in Galveston. In school months, that left only one son at home—me. The burden on Papa and Uncle Johnny was overwhelming.

"Be dogged!" Papa muttered, looking out at the Negroes, trying to orient his mind. He was bareheaded, graying hair tousled. "Sorry," he finally said to George Austin, "but we cain't do it. Hail ruined all the cotton, and even the corn is nothing much, and——."

"We ain't askin' no pay, Mistuh Will. We'll all make out, suh. Stop frettin yo' mind. You needs us, we needs work, you got some smokehouse"—he meant cured meats—"and some corn meal and stuff, and I shoots us all plenty squirrels, rabbits, birds, mos' likely a buck deer. Whoo, man, tha's eatin'!" He laughed happily.

His optimism, his outlook on life, was contagious. I myself had even been worried. Now suddenly I felt good. I saw Papa's eyes brighten a little, too. The black man went on. "Me, I'm name George Austin. In the wagon, she my wife Ellen. You and Miss Archie rest yo' minds. We take care things."

Mama had overheard it all. I saw her half rise from her rocker then sit back down. Her face, too, had lightened, and I knew what she was thinking; the Lord was answering some prayers.

George turned his smile from Papa and focused it on me. "Come on, Skeeter," he said. Then he caught my wrist in his powerful right hand, lifted me onto broad shoulders and jogged playfully away. He deposited me in the wagon seat and handed me the reins. Ellen chuckled and said, "Hi." George said, "I opens the gate."

The gate was at the end of the roadway up from that other gate down yonder beside the railroad. We often pastured our mules and horses in this big front lawn to help keep down the grass. Now I drove the guest team into our big area that held the two great red barns, plus a cowshed with its eight stalls.

George Austin was humming-singing softly as he beckoned me to stop the wagon under a big sycamore tree that shaded a sandy area there. *The little boy Jesus say to me, Come set heah under this big tree, An' let's learn how to git hap-pee . . . hum tiddy hum-tum tweedle de-dee——*. He broke the music with a sudden question. "How you been doin' in school and suchlike, Skeeter man, hunh?" He was unhitching traces, snapping them off the wagon singletrees.

I don't think I had ever felt more lighthearted; or ever have since. Instinct told me that I had a pal, a new friend. I fell to removing the breastyoke chains, a task really beyond my tender years and size, but George lifted the heavy wagon tongue so that I could do it easily. He made it casual, a cooperative effort with no embarrassment for me, talking all the while.

Meanwhile, Ellen was rearranging their few possessions in the wagon bed. George had said they'd sleep in the barn. He meant *at* the barn, or near it; specifically, now, under the great sycamore, which would keep off any dew and even turn a light shower. The couple had no wagon canvas. But I came up with a bright idea.

"Say, whyn't we go git us some soft hay to put under your quilts?"

Ellen beamed. "That would sho help," she admitted. "You a good friend, Skeeter. Yo' real name Oren, ain't it? From The Bible?"

I nodded. "First Chronicles 2:25." Uncle Johnny had learnt—taught—me that much. But I didn't care much for the name. I didn't know anybody else named Oren, and I disliked the feeling of being "different" because of it. Eventually I outgrew that. Today I know many Orens, even two other Oren Arnolds, no kin.

We got the hay and spread it in the wagon bed to make a truly comfortable mattress. Never mind about any modern super-engineered mattresses of suspension springs, foam rubber, plastics, air, or—heaven help us—even water. If you have never slept on fresh field hay with its delicate fragrance, its gentle sound as you turn over, you have missed one of the sweet, simple pleasures of life. I envied Ellen and George. Mama sometimes let me sleep on a quilt in the hay loft, just for fun, especially if I had a boy guest. But I can tell you that weird sounds could come up out there after midnight, and I never quite knew what made them. I'd be scared, but even more ashamed to come back to the house.

If rains had been threatening today, I would have urged Ellen and George to move their quilts to that loft. But under a rustly tree in a wagon bed is fun too, so I helped them spread. I noticed how immaculately clean their pitifully few possessions were, as clean as Mama's things in the house. Even the clothes they wore, though faded, were spotless, and there was absolutely no odor. Cleanliness, or lack of it, can proclaim people's personalities better than speech. Though I suppose it can be overdone.

We took the horses into the barn. I saw Papa still watching us from inside the yard, saying nothing. George and I shucked twelve ears of corn for each of his hungry horses and threw down big armloads of hay for the feed trough, which was four feet wide. When we slipped their bridles off, however, their first move was to trot out of the feeding shed, lie in the dry sand out there, and wallow with loud ploppings and gruntings. Then both stood up, shook themselves prodigiously, and walked to the barn-lot well nearby. Beside it was a heavy iron pot five feet across, a hollow hemisphere. The horses had smelled the water in it, but I started drawing more because the supply was low and warm.

George let me draw. He must have observed that I was straining, but he knew I had my pride. The beasts drank an incredible amount, belched, chomped, dribbled, drank some more, then made for the feed trough. Our own stock—six big mules, eight horses—were just beyond the fence in the pasture, glaring at their intruder guests feasting on gourmet corn.

Then I noticed that George had stopped still and was standing spread-legged, knuckles on hips, staring at the barnlot ground. A lot of fresh animal droppings rested there, with flies buzzing. I felt a twinge of shame. Normally we kept all manure picked up and placed in a corner bin with lime spread on it, to be put on the fields next winter. But in recent weeks everybody had just been too dog-tired to maintain standards. George seemed to understand. In ten minutes he had wielded the broad, many-tined scoop-fork so forcefully, had raked and "neated up" the place so tidily, that it seemed literally to shine. All the while he was humming-singing his little song.

In the 1960's and 1970's Adele, my beloved wife, and I have toured Europe repeatedly. In Germany we were impressed by the very neatly stacked scoops of manure, head high against the *front* walls of farm houses, nearest the streets or roads. I just had to inquire. Why there, rather than out in the barn lots where the smell wouldn't penetrate the homes?

I learned two things. One: Livestock often is housed under the same roof with its owners, though of course in separate rooms; thus the proximity, the odor, is unnoticed, or held inoffensive. Two: Over there, such a stack of manure is a status symbol; a mark of thrift and neatness, prosperity and distinction. We might meditate on that for hours, here. But no—for the benefit of moderns who tend to View With Alarm the smoggy emissions from automobiles, let us consider only one point: What if we had not developed the horseless carriage?

Can you envision a New York City, a Chicago, a Los Angeles, dependent solely on horses and mules today? Even in 1910 (and for centuries before, in all cities and towns), the streets in those places acquired a carpeting of fresh manure two inches or more thick before ten A.M. each day. The constant recurrence defied street sweepers; the acrid, offensive odor permeated our lives. Disease-carrying flies bred and swarmed by the astronomical billions, annoying us, sickening us, killing us. Stop damning the modern plague of automobiles.

Of course no such philosophizing entered our minds when George and I were in our barn lot that afternoon. Picking up the animal droppings was routine. Next thing I knew I was again piggyback on George's huge shoulders. He just swung me up there and trotted off, with Ellen chuckling and smiling. She followed us at a walk, and we entered Mama's kitchen.

"Don't make no noise, Skeet," George had murmured. "Yo' Papa and Mama, they 'sleep ag'in on the po'ch."

They were indeed, surprisingly, asleep on the porch, each on a cot. Papa snored happily. A new repose shone on Mama's face. I didn't understand it at the time. With newcomers here, how come they could go to sleep? I knew later, that they had simply let down, had relaxed in gratitude and trust. Nor was it ill placed. Ellen and George quietly prepared a good meal—called supper—in Mama's kitchen, which they had never seen before.

I cherish a vivid mental picture of Ellen in that kitchen, during the ensuing years. I can see her plumpness straining low into the barrel of flour, getting some on her black face, pouring a quart or so of it on the broad board that topped the barrel, mixing in lard and baking powder or something, and kneading biscuit dough, joshing me all the while. This was in the pantry, itself a rather large room. All manner of good things appeared in that room from time to time, in my boyhood; pies, notably. Not one pie at a time, but shelves of assorted ones, baked every few days. By today's standards, I am sure they were poor ones; the imperative "flaky crust" (an abomination, really, because it crumbles too easily) had not come into vogue in those years. Ellen's crusts were that same biscuit dough with a little more lard added. The pie as we know it in the 1970's is an American institution, refined. Almost all American people are children of Europe, yet Europe has no pies, compared to ours. Who "invented" American pie? At any rate, a smallish boy and his pals, or anyone of any age, could go cut himself a hunk of Ellen's pie any time he wished—fresh or dried peach or apple, raisin, huckleberry, blackberry—or grab a pocketful of teacakes, or a wedge of chocolate cake. Oh man, how good life was!

On that first night, Ellen made a pound cake and let me scrape the batter pan. Presently she said to me, "Go wake up yo' people, Skeeter man." Man, not boy; I was pleased. "Tell them to wash and come

to the dining room. You wash yo' ownself, too. Hear?" I came to
table scrubbed and shining. I had even combed my hair. Mama must
have been astounded. I kept my napkin properly tucked under my
chin. I sat up straight. I et—ate—without noise. I did not talk with
food in my mouth. Mama *must* have been astounded.

George and Ellen Austin. Negroes. Take-charge people. Illiterate.
God-fearing. Kind. Good-humored. Unbelievably poor, and unbelievably happy. I hope some of the black dissidents and protestors of
the 1970's are listening in here.

It was George who restored our farm manpower. With the big
sons now gone most of the time, Papa and Uncle Johnny had tried to
cope alone. Uncle Johnny even quit teaching to help us work.

On the next Sunday after his arrival, big George went down the
south wagon-road lane of our farm to the row of Negro cabins beside
a creek down there. He hired—no, conscripted, perhaps even impressed—two husky farm helpers to replace Papa's sons. Names, their
real ones. Biggon Hightower and Jackson Lewis. (Biggon died tragi-
cally about 1925. But in 1970 I visited Henderson, and found my way
into "Nigger Town" and into the home of Jackson Lewis. There Jack
lay, a coal-black skeleton on a clean bed, seeing me, unable to speak.
Remembering, he let tears stream, and reached for my hand. I took his,
and that of his wife, and briefly spoke to the Good Lawd for all of us,
sincerely but without undue emotion, secure in the Knowledge, sus-
tained by the Faith. A few days later, Jackson was gone.)

Those strong young men showed up at our barn before Monday
dawn, glad to work, with no talk whatever about hours or pay. Ellen
fed them breakfast. By six o'clock George had them already in the
field, plowing. He himself hung back. For a week now he had been
getting Ellen and himself "settled in," had greased all our wagons
and buggies, repaired and oiled the harness, sharpened the long many-
toothed mower blades with me endlessly and tediously turning the
heavy grindstone. He had built a new gate to the cowpen because a
bull had destroyed the old one. He had cut the bitterweeds all down
on the four acres or so of our front lawn, using the big mule-powered
mower, for which Mama blessed him. She had been trying to get those
weeds cut for weeks. He had rebuilt the well box on our porch, because the old one had rotted and was dangerous. He had split and

sawed at least a cord of stovewood for Mama's—now Ellen's—kitchen. So, all'in all, he had not yet got to the actual farmwork. But he had gone out to check on Biggon and Jackson several times. He found them conscientious workers.

This Monday morning it was slightly comical to watch Papa and Uncle Johnny. By instinct Papa was a take-charge man himself. For the past week he had sort of been marking time, getting acquainted, resting a lot. Uncle Johnny had busied himself picking ticks off our cows and mopping them with a smelly "soption," also dehorning a bull calf, with which task I helped. Today, though, the two white men stood there after breakfast and let George run the show. Papa was chewing Kiss-Me Gum, a nickle's worth at a time, as was his habit. He bought a fresh pack of it every Saturday, and the wad lasted him a week. Sometimes, rarely, I would be given one of the five little squares of freshly-bought gum. Papa took out his gum and fingered it when thinking. He had it out now.

"We is got things sort of cleaned up and ready, suh," George reported, hat in hand in deference, soon after breakfast this Monday. "This mawnin', I would sugges' that you and Mistuh Johnny just ride yo' hosses around and study things. See what all need most to be done in the fields, then come and tell me. All right, suh?"

If Papa resented his taking over, he did not show it. He knew the dire need; we had already muddled through stringent times, and in that era there was no such outrageous thing as government subsidy, no insulting welfare program on which bureaucrats could fatten. Papa was showing hospitality not only to a Negro couple, but to the whole idea of accepting kindly help from them as sent by his brother-in-law, Charlie Dawson. That took some doing; that required a humble, broad-minded, high-class man.

"All right, George," he nodded. "Yes, we'll talk here at noon, then."

"Thank you, suh. I look around the land my own self, this mawnin'. Kind of git things in my mind, like. After dinnuh, I gits to work, too." He meant after lunch, but the word lunch was not in our language. We had dinner at noon, supper at night.

From that point, my memory is somewhat spotty concerning black George and Ellen. Oh, endless sporadic bits return; incidents, snatches of talk, stretches of labor, happy moments. But no long continuity. Because my boyish ego was involved in it, I do cherish one memorable incident from that first year the Austins were with us. By that time George had hired not two but five black farm hands. They were needed because he had seen how run down things were, and how much the crop production might be increased. Thus Ellen began feeding all six Negro men in the big kitchen at a long table covered with checkered oil cloth. As a small boy I discovered that eating breakfast with those men was much more fun than eating with the whites in the dining room.

George himself sat at one end of the table, and he put me next on his right. One morning, with all the husky black help seated and smiling and joshing in anticipation, Ellen put a huge platter of fried beefsteaks on the table (we did not eat "breakfast foods" and such pap back there). The routine was to take a big steak onto your plate, pour thick homemade cane molasses all over it, criss-cross cut it into big bite-sized pieces, butter yourself a huge hot biscuit, then pitch in. Let city-dude ribbon clerks have their pheasant under glass; let me eat with the hands in that kitchen.

Well, on this particular morning a new Negro instantly reached with his fork and lifted a steak onto his plate. A split second later, George Austin's hamlike hand reached across me and slapped the worker in the face. George glared at him and said, "Man, does you evuh ag'in git yo'self a steak befo' Mistuh Oren gits hisn, does I knock you silly!"

I refrain from further comment, except to say that in the moment of hush that followed I felt a strange and powerful emotional reaction. Nothing further was said or ever came of it. Until I bawled at George's funeral years later.

In due time I found myself no longer as much a farm hand—I use the term loosely—as I was a cowboy. That was because Papa and George had expanded. With a lot of grassed woodland and open areas under fence, they had "gotten into cattle," so that before we realized it we Arnolds had, in the Texas fashion, become ranchers as well as farmers. We soon had four to five hundred head of steers to pasture, feed, dehorn, de-tick, brand, castrate, worry about, drive a mile to the depot, and load on slatted freight cars. Biggon and Jackson and the other helpers took to the saddle with true zest; history has not done justice to the Negro cowboys on our Western ranches.

My own cowboying was much more satisfying than my farming had been. Frankly, I hated that eternally monotonous planting of seeds, chopping and plowing, slinging of pitchforks, picking speckled peas and then the bolls of cotton, most of it under a scorching sun. Washington Irving wrote that "A man who bestrides a horse must be essentially different from the man who cowers in a canoe," and while farming admits no cowardice, I see eye-to-eye with Irving's romantic appraisal. Nuts to the drudgery of tillage. In the saddle it is heigh-ho and away we go, yip-yippee. I ask you, how many movies and TV shows do you see built around clod-hopping farmers?

I learned to spur my roan, Sassy, stand in my stirrups, and lasso a yearling bull. Man, that's living! Showing off on Sunday afternoons to my town-dude pals, who loved to visit at our place, I would run Sassy a seeming mile-a-minute (the accepted ultimate in speed in those years), swing low from the saddle, and pick a red bandana handkerchief off the ground. Hot dawg! The act went sour, however, when Bonny Flanagan and some other "female girls" were watching us one day. I may have had my attention focused more on blonde Bonny than on the red bandana. Embarrassingly, I had to lie in bed two days with a skinned scalp and a sprained back.

With a new prosperity apparently settled on the Will Arnold spread, we soon acquired an automobile, one of Henderson's earliest.

It was an Overland "Chummy Roadster." You stepped high twice to go in a front door, passed between two front seats, and sat in a doorless rear compartment if you were Important. Me, I clung up front near the controls. There was no top to this vehicle; presumably, it was not expected to be used in the rain, and if there is anything sillier than a dangerous rain-and-dust-catching "convertible" today, I haven't seen it, but back there such a thing was—I believe we said "the cat's meow," or possibly "the bee's knees" (though I am not exactly sure when those laudatory slang expressions originated). At any rate, our Chummy Roadster also sported a remarkable black bulb. Squeeze the thing, and everybody for a mile around heard the loud warning squawk of a gander. I could charge Negro boys and country white guests a marble or other trinket to squeeze that horn; unless

Papa was nearby. Sister Opal still has one of my agates obtained that way. She says she will give it to her new great grandson, Loren Schley, when he comes up to age eight or so. Sentiment is a force.

George Austin learned to drive that horseless carriage in short order. I hope God has given him one in heaven. No mere harp or other musical instrument, however celestial, could possibly have brought him more pleasure than borrowing our auto and driving it to a Negro picnic on a Sunday afternoon. Aye, that were paradise enow.

In retrospect, I see George only as an eternally happy, singing, laughing, hard-working man who big-brothered me more than my real big brothers did. But doubtless there were moments of man-to-man adjustments between him and Will Arnold. I can recall only one truly unpleasant episode, and it occurred several years after the Austins arrived. I never knew what lay behind it, or what triggered it.

I was then age fifteen or so, and eight of us workers were gathered for some reason near the farm blacksmith shop, where we made equipment repairs and shod our horses. For years my task there had been to pump the great eight-foot bellows which "blowed" air up from the bottom of the fire box through glowing coal that heated the metal to red or pinkish-white. This was fun, of course, and little Negro boys and even white guests often begged me to share the honor with them. Sometimes, when feeling magnanimous, I did so.

This morning I must have been inattentive to have missed the beginnings of drama just outside the door. First thing I knew, I heard Papa cuss. I stopped pumping, looked out, and saw him suddenly grab up a singletree. (Is there anyone in this audience who does not know what a singletree is? In effect, it is a heavy hickory club about thirty inches long with a dangling iron hook on each end.)

In what obviously was a moment of rage, Papa swung that club at his close friend and foreman, George Austin.

If hit on the head, George would have been killed by the blow, as Papa seemed to hope at that moment. It did not hit on the head. It did not hit at all. George merely swung backward out of range then quickly grabbed the singletree, twisted it out of Papa's hand and threw it aside. In the same motion his great black hands clamped like handcuffs around Papa's wrists.

"Mistuh Will, suh, oh Mistuh Will, suh, don' make me haff to hurt you, suh. Please, I asks you, suh." I remember his exact words, so greatly was I impressed.

The rest of us had frozen in horror. I recall how huge black Henry Murphy, naked to the waist, paused over his anvil there with hammer high, a giant in silhouette against the shop window. I let the bellows die in a slowly sighing breath. I stepped to the door, but no one else seemed able to move. Finally, when George Austin relaxed his grip, Papa's hands dropped to his sides. Our good dog Rags came close to the two men and whined, trying to lick each one. Nobody spoke, but I could feel my heart pounding. Papa might yet pick up that singletree or might go get a gun, or heaven knew what.

George walked over to Papa's horse that stood saddled nearby and put his head against the horse's mane, plainly a shaken man, striving for composure. Presently Papa walked slowly toward his friend. Would he strike the black man? Fight with him? Fire him from our employ? I wanted desperately to stop him, I wanted to do *something*. The drama held me spellbound.

But Papa simply murmured "George" and stuck out his hand.

George turned, and shook the hand, and I saw tears in *his* eyes matching my own, big capable he-man that he was.

"Mistuh Will, suh," he murmured.

Then George turned to the awestricken workers who were staring with open mouths and snapped at them. "What for you Nigguhs just standin' around heah doin' nothing? Git on about yo' work. Mistuh Will ain't payin you all to loaf. *You heah me?*"

He drew back an arm as if to strike all of them in one great blow. Whereupon all sprang into some kind of simulated activity. They had not yet been assigned any work this morning, but they made great pretense in a big hurry, acting as if nothing had ever happened. Big George had one more word for them:

"Does any one of you black devils evuh talk about this, does I my own self come ram my fis' down yo' thoat. Now *git!*"

We got. His awesome scowl also had taken me in, and I understood. I have never talked about the incident. Until right now.

The return of prosperity to our farm-ranch was coincidental with, and perhaps largely caused by, the advent of George and Ellen Austin. Papa was not articulate about it, but Mama said that welcoming the Austins had become bread on the waters. Ellen was far from any "black mammy" stereotype, George was never an "old Southern servant" personality. They were very near to being a part of our family; and let no reader take umbrage, no militant black, no fanatical white idealist crusading against "prejudice" here in the 1970's. There was never any oppression on our farm, no real class distinction. I do not blame intelligent blacks in the 1970's for seeking more dignity and respect than many have received. I admire most the ones who try to earn it rather than merely demand it.

George Austin earned his, with a great sense of humor and devotion to his work. He was well paid. He got forty dollars a month, plus "fringe benefits" (a term unheard of back there) such as free housing and farm-grown foods. The workers that he or Papa hired were happy with the going wage—"another day, another dollar." One dollar per *hour* of course would be an insulting offer to laborers in the '70's and the work day now is a bare eight hours at most. For George and all of us, the work day matched the sun day, or exceeded it. It started before six A.M. even in winter, with feeding and milking chores and such. In summer it ended when we trudged from the fields about seven-thirty P.M. and still had those chores to do again.

We have come a long way.

George and Ellen lived out their lives with us, until she died of cancer and he in an accident. We all had built them a home, painted white, down on the front corner of our land, right near that same railroad. That gave them status; prestige. George soon ruled the Negro population of our town—with fists when necessary, once or twice with a gun, which only he and Papa and Sheriff Joel Hale knew was not loaded. But more often with cajolery and tact.

He never learned to read or write. He didn't need such skills. Success in living is not necessarily dependent on what we call literacy or education.

 *To Love a Papist*

As I have indicated already, Mama's instinct for hospitality was as strong as Papa's. They never discussed it, or needed to. Here was a big white house on a hill with its doors open to everyone, and that was that. Mama's altruistic outreach soon extended thoughout the county-seat town, as well as the rural parts of the county.

Frequently she would hitch white Tom gelding to the buggy— which means that *I* hitched Tom to the buggy—and drive alone all the way back down to Minden, twelve miles, to visit her sister, Nannie McCarter, and bring Aunt Nannie back for a week's rest at our house. Aunt Nannie, frail at best, drove herself much too hard, trying to help Uncle Jim make ends meet.

It was wonderful to see Mama start that buggy trip. She was a ninety-eight-pound pink flower under a huge blue sunbonnet, sitting perkily in the buggy seat, clucking to Tom, and singing a little song as the big horse trotted off down the front lawn. It would take them four hours to travel the twelve miles to Minden, often through deep sand or in muddy ruts, up steep hills and down. She was completely unafraid. When she and Tom crossed the railroad and headed south, she would turn in her seat and wave back to us.

"You be careful!" Papa would shout. In such moments, I always wanted to cry. But I wouldn't have dared, with Papa and sister Opal and likely other people looking on; my preadolescent manhood would have been critically subverted. Once Papa did send me horseback to follow her "at a respectful distance" and see that no harm came to her. But shucks, she spotted me before she got to Town Creek, a mile south of the courthouse, waited for me, and ordered me back home. After that we just let her go. After all, there was no real danger; big Tom himself was a dependable escort. Once my brother Grady was coming home from Minden alone in a wagon, with Tom and a lesser horse in the traces. This was at night, and a mile out of Minden Grady lay down on some hay in the wagon and went to sleep. We found him asleep there at our side gate next dawn. Tom had piloted them safely for eleven miles.

Aunt Nannie, then, enjoyed our Big City home often, as escape from backwoods living. So did Aunt Evie, and Miss Daisy Barefield, and Mrs. Sinclair, and I can't think how many more country women. Yet it was in Henderson itself that Mama seemed to find the closest friends and show the most frequent open-house hospitality. It was routine for her to go to our hall wall telephone, ring up "central" and say "Hello, Agnes, how are you? . . . Yes, thank you, we are all well. Give me Wood's, please." Soon Mrs. Wood would come on the line, and the two would visit amiably, and Mama would invite her out to spend the day tomorrow. Mrs. Wood would gladly accept—and arrive at eight A.M., to depart at six P.M., so both could "set" and fan themselves with palm-leaf fans from Hightower's Drug Store and talk more happy woman talk. The fans were free, the conversation was broad in scope. Peace of mind? It cometh slyly. It came to Mama there.

It faded a little one morning when that same telephone rang. At first I paid scant attention; I was lying on the horsehair couch in the big hallway deep in *Paddle Your Own Canoe*, a wonderfully inspiring book by that Mr. Alger. I longed to paddle mine in life, and resolved to. (In some measure, so I have.) Wherefore, I paid no attention to the phone call until I heard Mama exclaim "Oh pshaw!" Plainly something serious had arisen.

Something had. A family of Catholics had come to Henderson.

Except for the Endels, who ran a clothing store, and the Marwils who ran a competing business, and Judge Brachfield, and the Wolfes, all of whom were known to be "good" Jews and were much respected, even loved, Henderson was one hundred percent Protestant Christian. Papa was Baptist. Mama was Presbyterian and saw to it that we five kids were. But Papa supplied big beautiful Christmas trees for each church each season, thick green holly growths brilliant with crimson berries, right off our farm. One year some brash Methodists dared snitch a tree he had marked in his mind for Baptist use. On horseback, he caught them and sternly made them tote it right on into the Baptist sanctuary and set it up in there. It made good chuckly town talk all that winter.

But there was of course no Catholic Church, so why had these heathen Papists dared come to our community? Thus the telephone gossip. It zipped around town that morning and got to Mama. With my ears erect now, I got the message that maybe a posse would be formed to drive them away. Oh, perhaps not with violence, but nevertheless with firmness.

"No, no, Matilda!" Mama was speaking to Miss Matilda Weems. That is, *Mrs.* Matilda Weems. In the land of Dixie, which includes Texas, "Miss" was, and still is, a term of respect used whenever men addressed a married lady and felt cordial enough to want to use her first name. It is a sweet custom. "No, no, I say. 'Tilda, it would not be Christian. Brother Hornbeak preached just a few Sundays ago on not thinking harshly of others. 'Judge not lest ye be judged.' If we are to take and despise everybody who—."

Miss Matilda must have interrupted, because Mama—and I—listened intently for several seconds. Miss Matilda, wrought up, spoke loudly enough for me to hear every word.

"Well you just tell them to hold off," Mama put in with asperity. "I will go right down there myself and talk with the family, then let the town people know. There is no need for haste."

With that she clapped the receiver back onto its hook and rang off. She had not noticed me, was unaware of my fascinated interest. She stood firm-lipped, thinking, then yelled, "*Oren!*" I was within three feet of her, so I wisely pretended I had been asleep. I sat up drowsily rubbing my eyes, yawned, and answered, "Ma'am?"

"Go hitch up Tom."

"You goin' to market?" That meant a grocery store.

"You hush and go hitch up Tom." I hushed and went to hitch up Tom.

Though I hinted, and finally begged, I was not allowed to accompany her. She was wearing her Archie Barry Arnold *look*. An Irish look. A gleam. A glint in her eye, purposeful, focused, determined.

I have not explained that odd name for a girl, Archie. Boys, not girls, are commonly named Arch, I believe. My grandfather, Archibald Barry, was killed far off in the East by a Yankee bullet; he never saw his little girl baby, who was born in a backwoods log cabin in Texas. Grandmother was so distressed, so sentimental, that she named their baby for him—Archibald Laetitia Barry. Somehow she got called Archie instead of Tisha or Tish. To feed her fatherless brood, Grandmother Barry would shoot deer from her tiny front porch, so rustic was their homeland. "Advantages?" There were none, in that horrible postwar reconstruction period. Small wonder Mama grew up unschooled, except in what are called the eternal verities learned at her mother's knee. One of them was a Christianity that required action, not merely a passive "faith."

Which is why she struck big Tom gelding on the rump, quite unnecessarily, with the buggy whip as she started down the big front lawn that morning. Tom looked back in astonishment and not a little indignation. All she needed to do was cluck to him, as both he and she well knew. He could not know about the Catholic emergency.

Two hours later, Mama walked Tom back up that front lawn guiding a big family in a big wagon, right behind her.

They all pulled up near that side gate. (Nobody ever used our front yard gate, except suitors calling on sister Opal.) "You all come right on in," Mama ordered.

It was noon then, so Papa and George Austin and Biggon Hightower and Jackson Lewis and two other hired Negroes were in the side yard, awaiting dinner. And I, too, of course; hungry, but even more consumed with wide-eyed curiosity.

Mama brought the troop of Catholics in—parents, seven children, even a Collie dog. Our Rags sniffed the newcomer and rumbled a warning, but Papa said "You go lie down!" so forcefully that Rags drooped his tail, slunk down the back kitchen steps and went into his bed of old potato sacks there beside the well box under the porch floor. I petted the guest dog, traitor that I was.

"Will, like to introduce the O'Reilly family," Mama began. The purposeful glint was still in her eye. She was in command.

Papa shook hands all around, very formally for him. Names, many names, were mentioned, with negligible talk and no smiling. Even the Negroes were introduced. They stood respectfully and murmured acknowledgments.

Papa took his cue from Mama's eyes and said firmly, "Proud to meet you folks. Son," he turned to me, "more chairs. And tell Ellen. Come and wash, folks, and have a cold drink of water. Dinner ready right shortly now." Papa asked no questions; he was biding his time. Mama and I were the only homefolk who knew who these strange O'Reillys were. I kept my mouth shut; wonder of wonders.

It was some thirty minutes before Ellen had enough extra dinner prepared, so we had time to start getting acquainted. Mr. O'Reilly eased the tension. After a proper interval of small talk, he made bold.

"Have to tell you, Mr. Arnold, that———."

"Will Arnold. Just call me Will."

"Proud to, suh. Will. Patrick here. Called Pat. Have to tell you, suh, that me and my folks are Catholics."

Papa didn't bat an eyelash. Not a Baptist muscle moved, until he nodded formally and said, "Baptist, here. My wife is Presbyterian. Her and me don't argue. *You* and me won't argue, Pat. Any man's religion is his own business."

Papa seemed nine feet tall to me when he said that, even if I didn't fully understand it. He sat very erect, his great Texas head tousled but somehow noble.

At that instant Mrs. O'Reilly burst into tears and covered her face with her hands.

"There now, Maria," Mama stood up, hand on the woman's arm, then led her on into the house, saying, "Oren, take the children into the yard and play hide-and-seek until Ellen calls."

As we trooped down the steps, I heard Mr. O'Reilly stand up and say to Papa. "Will, I'd like to shake your hand again, suh."

Back near the fence in the sycamore and honeysuckle shade, George Austin started singing-chanting: *The little boy Jesus say to me, Come sit heah under this big tree. . . .* The other darkies—we called them that, in respect—took it up, low tone, feelingly, meaningfully. I wanted to stop and listen. But I was first "it" in hide-and-seek, and my duties were cut out for me. I was conscious of the fact that I had no country-hick Deasons with me this time; those Catholic kids were as smart as I. Smarter, I feared. Somehow they just *looked* it, in their eager faces and subtlety of manner. I started counting, with my eyes buried in my arms against a sycamore tree that was Home Base. The seven O'Reilly children evaporated like a covey of bobwhite quail chicks.

All right, then. Each of us had his emotions under control by the time Ellen opened the kitchen screen door, fanned flies away with her apron, and shouted "DINNUH!"

We children did not break and run toward the dining room as kids in the 1970's do. We understood. That was another era, with different —and, very possibly, better—folk customs in many respects. We youngsters knew we had to wait for second table. Mama, Papa, the O'Reilly elders, sister Opal, and Uncle Johnny, took up six of the eight places in the big dining room. The Negro workers trudged in, famished, to sit around the long table in the kitchen.

I learned later that Papa asked Mr. O'Reilly if he would like to ask the blessing. He would. He prayed fervently, in thanks, ending with his ritual prayer. All the Catholics crossed themselves and said "Amen." Papa intoned "A-men," which was something *we* had never heard him do. I know he had to force himself there; praying was not his metier, at least not in public.

In my grinning juvenility I had assumed that these strange folk would have dinner with us, then be on their way. I knew they were not traveling but had moved to Henderson; obviously Mama had simply brought them home for a hospitable visit and feeding.

Not so. Mama knew well that her three big sons were away at college, hence three double beds were empty. Next thing I realized, the O'Reillys were moving into our house with us—Catholics or no! There was a great flurry of assigning beds, setting up extra cots, allotting covers, pillows, and such.

Me and two of their boys—that is to say, two O'Reilly sons and I —got the honor of bedding down on pallets in the parlor with Mama's incubator, which even then had 115 eggs in it, kept warm by a small kerosene lamp. I had to explain the thing to everybody, scientist that I was. Which also got us into the origins of *human* babies, and I was able to straighten out these small O'Reillys on that matter. I made it clear that the mama prayed for a baby, then God deposited one in a designated hollow stump near the home, and the mama would go there and get it—and wasn't that nice? We had no stork in our folklore; storks were unknown in this part of Texas.

Mama escorted Maria O'Reilly and three daughters down the eight kitchen steps, through the back yard gate, around the high pile of split stovewood, and down a path fifty yards behind some spreading

fig trees. We males pretended not to notice. But we knew that the
privy was down there. Its three holes, kept meticulously clean, made
affairs in there sociable, as required. Male members of our family
rarely ever used that facility, however; we simply "went to the barn."
Let any moderns meditate on those facts; especially any who tend to
get upset when their sparkling bathrooms are decorated in fuchsia
tints instead of a preferred lime green. Heaven help us.

I do not recall just how long those Papists lived with us. It must
have been something like two weeks. That was long enough for Pat-
trick and Will and the oldest O'Reilly boy and some volunteer helpers
from among the townsmen to repair and even paint a sturdy rent
house for the O'Reillys about half a mile from our own. That repair
and painting paid for the first two months rent.

One week the following winter Mr. O'Reilly paid us all back. He
happened to be standing with Papa in our barnlot one morning when
work was slack for our hands, and Negro Milus Lewis asked Papa if
he could borrow a team of mules and a dirt scraper.

"What for?" Papa naturally asked.

"We wants to level us off a lot down by the depot, suh," Milus explained, "so's we can maybe build us a Methodist Church on it a little
at a time."

Patrick O'Reilly spoke right up. "A little at a time? Why I am not
rushed now, and I've got a big son. Will, you've got hands loafing
around. What say?"

Papa nodded. Upshot was that we white Protestants and black
Protestants and those white Catholics all pitched in and not only built
but painted that First African Methodist Church in just six days. Then
on the seventh all gathered there for the dedicatory service. If a priest
or an archbishop or somebody disapproved of the O'Reillys' actions
I never heard of it.

I do remember that morning's sermon. The Negroes of the congre-
gation interrupted their preacher every few moments; or rather, en-
dorsed him. He would say, for instance: "We cain't go around bein'
selfish and mean, we has to love the Lord Jesus and do what *He*
done." Now that, of course, is marvelous, simple, elemental Christian
doctrine, and heaven protect us from ecclesiastical gobbledygook.
Right at that point, the black worshipers would bob their heads and

firmly intone, "A-men!" or "You is co-reck, Rev-rund!" or "Yes, suh, that is gospel truf!" or "Lawd, Lawd, fo-give me, a sinnuh!" Smile if you will. But don't let me see you do it.

At that time I did not fully appreciate all the human aspects, the subtler nuances and significances. But I did sense that the acceptance of the Catholics stemmed from the moment Mama got back to her telephone.

"Matilda," she spoke firmly, out of the O'Reillys' hearing, "you tell those hotheaded ones that these folks are not lepers, they are just like we are. Better in some ways, I vow. They had been camping down there beside Town Creek, sleeping on the ground, because nobody would rent them a house, much less give the man a job. You spread the word that me and Will have tried to help them." Mama hung up.

Miss Matilda may have demurred; I don't know. But if so, she lost. In a short while the whole town seemed eager to befriend the O'Reillys. Louellen O'Reilly became school valedictorian. Dennis, the eldest, went on up to own the blacksmith shop and converted it into a garage for repairing motor carriages.

As for the prettiest one, Mary-Margaret Sara O'Reilly, just my age, I fell desperately, overwhelmingly in love with her. It lasted until I was into my fifteenth year.

Maybe it's just as well that I was Presbyterian.

The O'Reillys accepted us even as we accepted them. Soon there was no more "feeling" about the differences in religion, no more references to it in anybody's conversation. Their children played often at our place and all of us enjoyed that.

One beloved game was "Soldiers." We would divide up into Yanks and Confeds, one group would take the barn loft as a fort, and the enemies would attack it. Our ammunition? You must allow me to be indelicate here, because we used halves of corncobs, and these had already been trampled into the manure of the barnlot, hence were quite heavy and "throwable." If you threw one of these things and hit, not only would it splash a bit, it would hurt. If you did get hit, you were "dead" and out of the game.

Mary-Margaret Sara hit me once when I was an attacking Reb on the ground. Dramatizing it (I was ever a great ham), I fell down, writhed in agony, and pleaded for help. Benson Alford, Bubba High-

tower, black Cleveland Lewis (we had no qualms about letting the
Negro children play with us), and Tunk Griffin, my coattackers, ignored my showing off.

But Mary-Margaret Sara beheld me writhing in the throes of death
and promptly jumped out the high loft window. We had thought-
fully put a pile of hay down there for just such an emergency, hence
she landed safely. She ran to me and knelt over me. I moaned. "Oh,
Oren," she cried, "are you really hurt badly? Please don't be."

Never mind what came of that! Love is love, and private, see. But
it happened that Ellen Austin saw it all from our kitchen porch, where
she was resting in a chair. Later Ellen said to me, "That Miss Mary-
Margaret Sara, she might nigh nice as you is. Nicer, maybe, Hunh?"

Yes, nicer. I well recall.

 # The Egg-Bought Shoes

Try as I will, I can not recall when, why, or how Uncle' John and Aunt Rachel Harris came to us.

Somewhere along the line of years they were just *there*; living in a very small four-room unpainted house on a slope below a spring about a mile behind our white mansion. I feel quite sure that Papa or Mama brought them there. Because the Harrises were "old folks" and, so far as I knew, always had been. I do recall clearly that we used to visit them in that old home village of Minden, whenever we would drive back down there to call on our kin. John and Rachel were not relatives of ours, but everybody called them Aunt and Uncle out of love and respect. They deserved every ounce of that.

My mental picture of them creeps into focus somewhere around 1910, and it is not like the color TV screen; it is in black-and-white. They were white folks, their heads even whiter. Their clothing seems always to have been gray, against the weathered gray of the house we gave them, and the setting of the house was—in my mind now—made largely white by the thick growth of open cotton bolls in the field around trees that shaded their cottage. Yet somehow it all added up to beauty, like that of an etching. I grew up realizing that the Harris couple represented yet another example of my parents' hospitality, their open-house hearts. Uncle John and Aunt Rachel were critically poor; but for us they could have starved.

Once I happened in on them real early. I had been riding Sassy across the fields, looking for an old sow that had broken out of her pen, and I stopped at the Harris place for a drink of well water. They were just having breakfast—of corn grains, parched on their stove. Nothing else. Offered some, I ate them. Tasty enough, and even nourishing. But I felt sick inside. I found where the old sow had birthed her piglets under some persimmon saplings and saw she was safe enough there, so I high-tailed Sassy on back home and reported about the Harrises. "Pshaw!" Mama berated herself. "We should have guessed."

So we fed them. Kept them stocked with meal and lard and hog meat from our farm; also sweet potatoes, cantaloupes, watermelons, plums, peaches, grapes, and strawberries in season. And sugar.

It all had to be handled with great care; pride is a powerful force among the Johns and Rachels of this earth, and a body would rather starve than lose it. Mama and Papa and Uncle Johnny and brother Tip and I conferred. I got in on it because I had discovered the need. The talk lasted half an hour or so.

"All right, then," Papa ended it by standing. "I will ride over there and tell Uncle John that I need help with my harness. I will say that Johnny Barry, here, is very busy getting some school work ready, and I need help oiling and repairing our harness. I will go in the wagon and bring Uncle John back. Rachel too, if she'll come."

"You make her come," Mama ordered. "Sweet talk her. Say that I am lonesome. I *am* lonesome. I need woman talk."

So Uncle John Harris was "hired" for a dollar a day, three days a week. That money was a godsend for a man crowding age eighty.

"It's a dollar a day and found," Papa then explained to Uncle John offhandedly, and succeeded in selling that idea too. Which enabled us to keep them supplied with food while saving face.

A difficulty arose about their water supply. First, I learned that it was very painful for either of the old people to draw up a bucket of well water, due to acute "rheumatics"—which today I suppose we would call arthritis. So, whoever among us happened to be near, would draw up several buckets for them to keep covered with a moist cup towel, which cooled it by evaporation. Then be dogged if their well didn't unaccountably go dry. Wells can do that, in the mysterious phenomena underground.

Big brother Tip Arnold, though, was touched with genius. He heard about the well, went over there, looked down in it, squatted on his hunkers—that is, his heels—and studied the matter silently. Uncle John and Aunt Rachel and I all remained silent; we respected a man doing serious thinking. Presently he stood and squinted across the cotton rows toward that spring slightly uphill from the Harris cottage. The spring was some two hundred yards away. Water could be toted from it, but that distance, for real old folks——.

"Nothing to it!" Tip suddenly snapped, grinning. "Be fun. Oren, go hitch a mule to that smallest scraper and drag it over here. Get old Toby, he's gentle. Two shovels. An axe. Uncle John, you already got a hammer and saw here, haven't you? And some nails? Plenty of planks on your pile of lumber out back. Come on, sir."

So, with barely a day's work, we diverted the cold water from that spring. By suppertime it was running along a new path scraped across the cotton, right to the Harris kitchen itself. There it flowed through a wooden trough into a catch basin that Tip and Uncle John had designed around an old iron wash pot holding maybe fifty gallons; thence overflowed and channeled itself on back into its original bed.

"It is a God's wonder!" Aunt Rachel declared.

It was indeed. Sheer luxury. Running fresh cold water, night and day the year round. We rarely had weather that would freeze even a pond, never a stream. Clean pure water right into the home itself! Status! Prestige! Not to mention convenience.

In April of 1973 I went back to visit Henderson, and had lunch in a fine restaurant owned by "Buddy" Dawson, grandson of that Uncle Charlie Dawson, Papa's brother-in-law. A new freeway ran in front of the restaurant. Standing out front, watching the traffic, I managed to orient myself. That modern eatery was on almost the exact site where the old Harris cottage had stood sixty years ago. New motels, garages, filling stations, shops, were all around; the rows of white-bolled cotton were missing. But a little stream of spring water was in evidence, and two dignified old hickory trees were getting their new spring foliage. I felt forlorn; old.

We had other minor troubles with water, in those years. Uncle John himself was wise—but not wise enough. He was called into consultation with Tip and Papa, and me a tagalong, about a messy situation near our pond. We had dammed up some springs nearer the home, at the lower edge of a pasture. It made a good place to go fishing, boating, and even swimming, although we seldom swam; a "swimming pool" was not the status symbol then that it is today. Anyway, that pond water too often had an oil slick on part of it. Uncle John Harris was the one who pointed out its source and passed final judgment on it. I well recall. I was standing right there at the time, hands in hip pockets, feeling mannish myself, thus to be associated with the grown men.

"Will," said Uncle John, "there ain't nothin' you can do. That there's just a natchel oil seep. Some black stuff, which ain't good for nothin', just keeps oozing out. You can't stop it. Best thing is just to fence it off so's the hogs won't wallow in it and git all greasy like."

Tip had a hoe in hand. He slogged over there through the mud, chopped down four or five times at the point of the oil seepage, and got more oil. "Damn," he said. Tip was given to cussing at times. He stood back, scowling, mopping his sweaty face. We all stared. A pesky nuisance, there.

So we fenced the area off to keep the hogs out of it.

I wish I could forget the matter. But, in this materialistic age, I can't. Here in 1974, I am still seeing reruns of a popular television series called "Beverly Hillbillies," in which a very backwoodsy gent happens to shoot a shotgun into just such an oil slick as ours was. I think he was aiming at a rabbit, but no matter, it's fictional anyway. When his charge strikes that oil slick, oil gushes; a real stream of the black, slimy stuff. Next thing we know, that fictional hillbilly is worth fifty million dollars!

Ours wasn't fictional. Within a very few years oil wells around Henderson, Texas, were gushing over their derricks, and the new field was worth not fifty but nearer five hundred million, maybe more. And Papa had sold his farm, without retaining mineral rights! All of us Arnolds could have been "filthy rich." What was it, again, that fellow Whittier wrote a century or more ago? "Of all sad words of tongue or pen the saddest are these, 'It might have been.'"? But oh well, as the born loser says today, I've et.

Rent-free hospitality and contrived groceries were not the extent of our hospitality shown Uncle John and Aunt Rachel Harris. I think also of clothing, especially shoes.

Citizens in our modern affluent society can hardly hope to appreciate the real value of shoes. They are taken for granted, as is the fine car, the expensive television set, the swimming pool. But away back yonder in our farm-ranch years, we appreciated, we cherished. Shoes were a God-given luxury. I could not count the days I walked or ran to school barefoot, simply because I had no shoes at the moment, or at least none I cared to risk in the rough and tumble of schoolground play. All of us guarded our shoes.

Then when any member of the family wore out a pair, with shrinkage and cracks and turnovers so bad as to make them uncomfortable, we developed the habit of tossing them under the steps that led down to the floor and tub in that back-porch bathroom. The result was that we usually had a pile of unlovely footgear gathering dust down there, both male and female.

That became a treasury for the colored folk. The word got around that any Negro—or any white person, for that matter—could go to Mr. Will and Miss Archie Arnold's back bathroom door, open it without asking permission or feeling embarrassed, and rummage out some kind of old shoes to wear. Furthermore, Mr. Johnny Barry kept a supply of his soot-and-suet shoe blacking in an old bucket there.

If the only pair you could get on was a mite tight, you had only to slit some holes in the upper leather with a pocketknife to enjoy comfort. This is a custom still in use; sometimes even new store-bought shoes are slit for comfort.

Once, in a welter of 12-year-old sentimentality, I gave my only pair of shoes to black Cleveland Lewis, my age. At first, Mama scolded me. Then she sniffed a bit, hugged me, took me downtown to Mays and Harris Store, and bought me new shoes on credit. Mama hated debt of any kind, so her egg money paid for those shoes within a few weeks. When the last of the entire $3.75 (Mama always bought good quality, even if it cost more) had been paid, she lectured me. I thought it was going to be about giving my first shoes away, but it wasn't; it was about buying on credit.

"Now, Oren"—she was firm-lipped—"you just take and learn

something here. You learn to save up the cost of anything before you buy it. What if I couldn't have sold enough eggs to pay for your new shoes? Where would you be, I ask you?"

I gave it my best thought, and said nothing. As far as I could see I'd still be right here, and the sky would not have fallen. I must have put on my stupid look—I was good at that—because Mama said "Fiddle!" and walked away.

But Uncle John Harris had overheard that moment of discipline, and quietly, as man-to-man, he explained that debt, any *debt*, can be a millstone around a person's neck. And, by George, it can! Somehow kindly old Uncle John got through to me. I have hated debt to this day, and seldom allowed it. My Adele and I have always tried to "save up the cost of anything *before* we bought it." This applies to furniture, clothing, cars, vacation trips, whatever. We have carried few millstones. Today I have several high-level banker friends. They tell me that the curse of materialistic young married Americans is indeed debt, especially installment buying, the "easy payment plans," and the plague of credit cards. Uncle John knew.

About my new egg-bought shoes, I will say in passing that they were not conventional black; wonder of wonders, they were high-toned tan. The whole family ohed and ahed over them, including Uncle John and Aunt Rachel. Best of all, George Austin also acquired some tan ones about then, and he came home with a bottle of red shoe dye. *Red*, mind you! He dyed his; his'n as he said. Unmistakably, they were gorgeous. So he offered to dye my new ones too. It was risky, but I agreed. Why not live a little, why not defy parental control once in a while? I was already feeling my oats, as the saying was. What I mean is, I was now into my teens, my glands were stirring, and I should do my own thinking.

You can forget about such modern trivia as costume coordinates, ensembles, matching or complementary footwear, trousers, shirts, ties, scarf loops, wide or narrow lapels, all that. I had new red shoes! When I showed up in Sunday school with them, I glowed, and not from Christianity. When next week I went to Mary-Margaret Sara O'Reilly's birthday party, I, not she, was the belle of the ball. Or so I felt. I wore them in Sassy's saddle back through the trees and the persimmon thicket and the cotton rows to show them to Aunt Rachel

Harris. "I ain't never seed the like of it!" she declared, hands lifted, then clasped before her breast in wonder, while Uncle John chuckled. We were on their front porch. She fed me a bait of molasses cookies, than which there is no finer eating this side of paradise.

So then Uncle John "took and made" me a little leather purse in which to put my coins, if ever I managed to save any, and said I could have George Austin dye that red too. Later that season—March, it must have been—he also whittled me some sticks for a kite that flew "a mile high" and showed me how to adjust its tail for proper length and balancing. Few kids today know how to do that.

I mentioned Aunt Rachel's molasses cookies. Her recipe has somehow come down through the decades, so that I am still addicted to them—"hooked on" them, I believe is the youth term today. Aunt Rachel's culinary skill was broadscreen. She could make a good meal out of next to nothing. Hominy, for instance, and turnip greens. The former must be made as she made it, to be truly delicious. She started —believe it or not—with ashes. I never knew the exact procedure, but somehow ashes boiled with flinty grains of field corn developed a lye, which in turn "ate out" the soft, undesirable core of each grain. Washed and reboiled, the grains then became delicious hominy. Comparably, fresh young turnip greens had to be picked just right and boiled with a hunk of salt pork. Put the two on a dinner table, add a tall glass of buttermilk, cooled in the well or the spring, finish with a stack of those cookies—oh, man! I have reason to suspect that Aunt Rachel, in her isolated cottage, and Ellen Austin, in our home kitchen, never heard of monosodium glutamate or any such. But don't misunderstand me; I am not as old-fashioned as I often pretend. My modern wife does understand monosodium glutamate, and her cooking is wonderful.

That gets me back to shoes.

On a certain Christmas Eve, Aunt Rachel, lacking money to buy me a store present, walked to our house and slipped a wrapped parcel of her cookies into my right shoe after I had gone to bed. No doubt my stocking was already filled. But that night somebody carelessly moved the leather shoe too close to the fireplace coals. The leather shrank, then charred, destroying the shoe.

We never told her. We just thanked her profusely for the cookies, though they, too, had been ruined by the heat. The shoes were a loss, yes, but not enough of one to spoil a Christmas. Papa must have been prospering that year, for I had *two* pairs of shoes. No, I did not believe in Santa Claus, literally; I was too old and sophisticated for that, at my ripe age. But I still hung up my stocking.

It was that same Christmas day on which George Austin, now firmly established as our work foreman, showed up in our back yard with Uncle John Harris. Their own open-house hospitality, their own kindness endorsing Papa's and Mama's, was showing. I was warming myself by the kitchen stove when I heard voices in the back yard. I went out and found those two men with a barefoot family of Negroes.

Uncle Johnny Barry was there, too, already rummaging in that bathroom bin of castoff shoes. I figured something was afoot—that's not meant to be funny—so I rushed into Mama's room, where she and Papa were sitting before the big warm fireplace, and told them about the people out back.

When Papa and Mama got there, Mama exclaimed, "Oh pshaw!"

The Negro family not only was barefoot on a freezing day, but had on negligible clothing. There were six of them; four children and parents. The smallest, a girl about eight years, wore only an empty burlap "tow" sack that had once held potatoes A hole in its bottom and sides admitted head and arms. I saw her shivering. Mr. Harris looked at Mama and Papa with pleading in his eyes. But he had confidence; he had known what to do when he came onto this black family.

Mama ordered me to saddle up my horse and get going while she went to the telephone. Papa led the black family into our kitchen for warmth; Ellen fed them, and George outfitted all of them with usable shoes that Uncle Johnny Barry had blacked. Uncle Johnny had to "peg" one pair to make it do. He had a shoe repair outfit; last, hammer, cutters, nails, awl, sewing thread, and leather scraps. Meanwhile, I galloped my horse over to Mrs. Flanagan's. She was Bonny's mother, who lived about half a mile on the other side of our peach orchard, was the postmistress of Henderson, and had a "passel" of fatherless kids at home. Mama knew she would have castoff clothing, even some of the late Mr. Flanagan's.

I came home with a great bundle of it, along with a bag of toys and candies. Before noon we had the happiest Negro family in Texas on our hands. George and Ellen Austin housed them until George could get the man squared away on a work project to earn his keep, and get into a small rent house. Santa Claus! I think he was a magical composite of white Uncle John Harris and black George Austin that Christmas. Incidentally, there was no great "to do" about the events of that day, no sentimentality, no embarrassment for anybody. Some poor folks, poorer, even, than Uncle John and Aunt Rachel, had needed shoes, and were brought to our back yard in faith. That's all there was to it.

I think of the occasion whenever I buy myself a new pair of shoes. I bought my most recent pair at Harrod's in London for something like thirty-five dollars, heaven forgive me! As I walked out to the street wearing them, my mind harked back sixty years or so. I carried my castoffs under my arm, and that night gave them to a porter in London's fashionably small and choosy Goring Hotel. "You are silent and introspective tonight," my Adele mentioned. Truly, I was.

In 1970 I took my eldest daughter, Judy, to the Maple Grove Cemetery, under the beautiful trees a mile from still backwoodsy Minden, the village whence we Arnolds and Harrises had come. There I showed her small, eroding stone markers that said John and Rachel Harris. Papa put them there. I hope my chances of being in heaven are even half as good as Aunt Rachel's and Uncle John's.

CHAPTER SIX

Honeybee's Sin

Now I must tell you—with an inevitable stirring of excitement and, I suppose, romance in my heart—about Honeybee.

Honeybee. Is anybody really named Honeybee? Why not! A honeybee is, all factors considered, a lovable, or at least admirable, creature. It works hard and minds its own business, which is more than a lot of human beings do. It produces something clean and good. But it is not helpless, not defenseless—annoy it and you'll find out! So, a good name for a girl.

But let's begin at the beginning, which means another brief look at that character in my life named Will Arnold. I have told you how George Austin "emancipated" himself by making himself our farm-ranch foreman. George's instinctive knowledge of how such an enterprise should be run proved priceless. By the end of his second year with us, Papa was out of debt and "getting ahead," so that he started getting ideas. One of them was put into his mind by his close friend, Mr. Joel Hale, the sheriff of our Rusk County.

"Will," the sheriff said, over half a cooled watermelon on our back porch, "dang it, we need a tax assessor. Only man who is threatening to run this time is a dad-danged Republican."

Moreover, the man was not only a Republican, he was a Methodist. So my prominent Baptist Papa ran for tax assessor and everybody else backed off.

I did not personally see much of his work in office because I was too young. But it became legendary, still is remembered by a few elders of the county. All I remember is that Papa was gone from home much of the time, 'sessin' tax. I often wondered just exactly what taxes were, and why we white people bothered with them. I had been reading about Indians in America, and no mention was made of taxes in their lives, which seemed to me to be very fine ones. And as for 'sessin'— I couldn't figure that out at all. Not that I really tried, or cared, at that fun-filled time of life.

However, I eventually learned that Papa's technique was to ride up to the home of a farmer, say, in some remote corner of Rusk County, call "Howdy!" from his saddle, and announce who he was. After a proper interval of discussing the state of the weather, the stand of cotton and corn, the birth—and likely the death, in that era of high infant mortality before germs were invented—of a new baby, Papa would say, "You are Sebe Travis. Sebastian Travis. Plot Six-A, of the Old Trammel Trace. Ain't that right, sir?"

Mr. Travis, standing in his yard, would nod, "That's right, Mr. Will."

"Well, how much taxes do you figure you ought to pay for 1912?"

The farmer would give earnest thought to that, then reply, "Oh, I think maybe about ten dollars would be fair."

"All right, I'll put you down for ten dollars, Sebe. You got only forty acres here, plus a house and barn and four mules, so that's reasonable. Like to have a drink of water, please sir."

"More'n that, Mr. Will. It's comin' on night. You'll sup and sleep here, and breakfast."

Whereupon Papa would swing down. He had expected it, even counted on it. Any stranger, especially a Man of Distinction, such as a tax assessor, would be an honored guest who could assuage the whole Travis family's hunger for contact with the outside world, for conversation and a general lift of spirits. Loneliness has ever been the bane of farm life. It has made neurotics of many an otherwise normal person, women especially.

That's the way it was, back then. I stand in awe, seeing the tax structure, the government machinery and bureaucracy, the incredibly computerized complication and wastage of the 1970's, the utter lack of personal feeling. Awe, and sadness, and nostalgic yearning. This was unwittingly expressed for me recently when my seventeen-year-old granddaughter Robin put a record on her stereo machine, and a fellow —Robert Goulet, I think it was—started singing: *Those were the days, my friend. We thought they'd nev-er end. . . .* Dear God.

It was on one of Papa's tax assessing journeys, rain slicker rolled behind his saddle, black record notebook inside his coat, that he happened onto the very pore—not poor, *pore*—family whom I shall call Phelps to avoid embarrassing people still living. Mama, sister Opal, Ellen, none of us at home ever knew exactly how matters developed in the distant Phelps household. The family, Papa said later, lived in piney woods four miles from the village of Shiloh, which of itself was nothing but a tiny store and six houses. Mr. Phelps was a sandy-land farmer, a one-gallus, good-hearted, but woefully ignorant and inept citizen whose only pleasures in life were begetting children and fishing.

When Papa returned home that weekend in a rainstorm, we saw his fine horse Dandy plop-plopping up the lawn with him, and there seemed to be a large hump on his back. "How come he ain't got on his slicker?" I remember asking.

"Isn't," Sis corrected, incorrectly, absent-mindedly, staring. She and Mama were "bound and determined"—the idiom of the region—that I should not grow up talking like Niggers. Negroes.

We stood on our covered side porch, studying him through the silver tapestry of the rain. Then, when Dandy stopped at the side gate, we saw that the hump was another person on the saddle apron. Papa got down, awkwardly, then half lifted the other person off. With both heads ducked against the downpour, they hastened onto the shelter of the porch. Papa's slicker had been over the second person.

We waited, staring in silence. Himself dripping copiously, soaked to the skin, Papa shook water off the slicker as he removed it, touched the second person and said, "It's all right, Honeybee child. Nothing wet but your legs and shoes. Archie, this here is Honeybee Phelps. And Opal, our only daughter. And this my son Skeeter. Name's Oren. Is there any hot coffee or suchlike?"

He didn't have to tell us. Surely he didn't have to tell me. We knew, for a certainty, that the house was open again, the hospitality policy was still in operation. Will Arnold, husband and father, was simply performing true to character and precedent established over the years.

By all the rights and precedents of fiction, any fifteen-year-old girl-child of the wilderness should be a paragon of femininity, a slender Perfection, tripping in diaphonous veils through springtime daisy fields. But this is not fiction, and that was September, and I have a somewhat less poetic memory of Honeybee as she was in that moment of arrival at our house on the hill.

She was trembling, and not just from rain chill. Her chin was on her chest, her face hiding behind stringy, drippy hair. I wouldn't have been surprised if she had sulled. Does anyone in the 1970's know what *sull* means? It seems to have no place in our modern, too-urban vocabulary. I cannot find it in the dictionary. But it was a convenient and expressive colloquialism back in the Good Old rural Days, at least Down South where 'possums lived.

When you went 'possum huntin' and your dogs treed one on a persimmon tree limb, you could shake the tree or limb and he'd fall to the ground and sull. Which is to say, the 'possum would "die" right there. Die dead, to all intents and purposes. He would be completely inert, limp, gone. You could pick him up by the tail and think the fall had killed him. The dogs would rush up, stop suddenly, sniff, then back off, satisfied that they had effected a kill. I never did understand the phenomenon. Likely it was, is, nature's way of allowing the perky little animal to protect itself. Maybe it exudes an odor that deceives the dogs into thinking it really is dead, or maybe it just goes into shock from fright. I ought to do some research on it, and I will, when I get around to it, I have promised myself for half a century. At any rate, leave the creature alone for, say, five or ten minutes, and all of a sudden it will jump up and run away! Isn't that something?

Honeybee didn't sull, but no doubt she would have liked to. No doubt she would have run all the way back to her shack home four miles from Shiloh if she could. And I am sure she had the physical stamina to do it, for she was healthy and strong. And proud. But frightened now. Mama put an arm around her and said, "Come on, darling," and Honeybee started sobbing.

Half an hour later, when we all sat for supper, silent Honeybee's head was erect and her face was pure pink marble, frozen in determined self-control. Two minutes later Mama kicked me under the table. I stopped staring at Honeybee and applied myself to fried chicken and cornbread with gravy poured over it. I was suffering no punishment except the indignity of being kicked. As I bowed over my plate to shovel in nourishment, I could still cock my eyes upward and look at Honeybee.

She was tallish enough, maybe, for sixteen. She wore a hideous faded dress thing of wasp-nest gray. I feel sure, now, that it had been handed down from her mother, poor soul, who must have worn it for ten years herself and likely still needed it. Honeybee had no stockings, doubtless possessed none. Her shoes, which had been sopping wet, now rested under the kitchen stove, where Ellen tended them. They were men's castoff high tops. Old, scuffed, ripped, with cracks and turned-up toes, and holes the size of quarters in their soles.

She never wore those shoes again. Ellen burned them, because it was discovered that Honeybee could wear a pair of sister Opal's, which, by contrast, were store-bought new in appearance. Honeybee beheld them with such obvious astonishment and pleasure that I thought Mama herself would do some sobbing. Honeybee did not speak her thanks. She only looked at them, at Opal and Mama, and at Papa in turn. She ignored me. Dang it. But then, I was negligible, as her younger brothers must have been.

Honeybee had come to live with us and get some schooling.

Surprisingly, she already had some. It developed that an itinerant preacher had discovered her four years earlier and had taught her to read, write, and cipher. She had taken to it so eagerly that he brought her many books, in increasing intellectual levels. Upshot was that she had what amounted to an elementary school education, though that still wasn't much in that decade in Rusk County, Texas. I remember that scholarly Uncle Johnny Barry tactfully tested her, then told us, out of her hearing, that she was much smarter than Oren.

That made me so mad that I slunk out and trotted past our big old pine Hanging Tree—a murderer had been hanged there before we moved to Henderson—and on to the pond, where I had left a line in the water tied to an overhanging willow limb. Lo, when I got there, the limb was bobbing up and down. Ignoring the boat, which was tied yonder by the dam, I clum—climbed—that tree and pulled up a goggle-eyed perch nearly as long as my forearm.

That offset the insult about Honeybee. So I ran back with my fish, placed it on the back porch near the kitchen door, and ran into the house to call everybody to come and look. When they came, dang if the fish wasn't gone. Search revealed that our mammy cat, old Susie, had grabbed it and taken it far up under the front part of the house, which was barely a foot off the ground, too low for me to get at Susie to kill her with a baseball bat, as I fully intended. I cried some in frustration and anger. At supper I was sullen. Nobody paid me any attention.

Honeybee's literacy was enough that Mama and Papa decided they should at least give her a tryout in high school. They talked to our friend, "Professor" Percy Bittle, about it. He was the school superintendent. He was my personal friend, too. He even taught me to play tennis, on his grassy lawn. I hope he is in heaven now; I bet he is. So the kindly man opened his high school to Honeybee.

Because this was already early September, school would "take up" in less than three weeks. The realization struck me with apprehension and horror, there at the breakfast table one morning. I myself was due to enter high school this fall. Obviously it would be my bounden duty, common courtesy, decreed by my no-nonsense parents, not only to escort this backwoods creature to school but also to "introduce her around."

I considered immediate departure. For the Navy. Maybe if I lied a little, being tall, they would let me in. I could run off and make my way to Galveston and enlist and help lick Kaiser Bill, which I had been yearning to do anyway. Then if I got blowed up by a submarine and died a horrible, lingering death in the cold, cold Atlantic, they would all be sorry. Likely they would have a memorial service in my honor at the Presbyterian Church, as prior heroes had already been honored. Brother Hornbeak himself would do the talking. And all the rest of their lives my parents would regret that they drove me to premature destruction by trying to force me to squire a danged old girl around at school.

In barely five days she had made me her slave.

My servitude began on her first Sunday, when we were getting ready for church and I saw that Mama and sister Opal had worked a miracle. Honeybee's long, stringy, dull hair was no longer long, stringy, dull hair; it was a put-up, shining, crowning glory. Don't ask me how this came about; no mere male ever understands such things, no male that masculine males respect, I mean. I did catch a glimpse of sister Opal hanging curling irons in her lamp chimney and, naturally, I poked my nose into her bedroom. But Sis turned wrathfully on me, snarled, "Twenty-three skiddoo," and I skiddooed.

Come to think of it, that was devastating persiflage, for the first decade of this century, Twenty-three skiddoo. It meant get lost, scram, blow, cut out, drop dead, disappear. I read just recently, I mean in the 1970's, that intense research has not revealed why we said "Twenty-three." The slanguage of yesteryear is a fascinating study all its own.

But there must have been more to it than a little hot hair curling. The hair was coal black, so that in sister's last-spring dress, cut down just a little, Honeybee looked like the pink blossoms that real honeybees sought. When she walked toward our Overland Chummy Roadster that morning, I gulped. I felt my heart action step up, and I diverted my eyes. I sat erect at the steering wheel—Papa had not yet learned to drive a horseless carriage—while the three ladies got in and walked to the rear. Mama and sister chatted. Honeybee was suffused with queenly silence.

Church attendance must have been a success that morning, though I have no idea what Miss Clieo Day, the Sunday-school teacher, or Brother Hornbeak, the preacher, said; my mind could not be refocused. The whole truth was, my sister Opal was undeniably the prettiest girl in Henderson, what with her two deep dimples and her bright all-encompassing smile. Dozens of suitors attested to it. Now here was a younger girl who almost matched her, and she would be living with us, and she was no kin to me! I abandoned all thoughts of running off to join the Navy.

About a week later I happened onto Mary-Margaret Sara O'Reilly. Somewhat forlornly she asked, "Oren, do you still like me?"

"Shucks," I said, and scuffed the toe of my left shoe with the sole of my right, "Why'd you ask a old question like that?"

At that moment, in fact all of that first two or three weeks of Sep-

tember, I *didn't* like Mary-Margaret Sara. My psyche had centered on the wilderness sprite from four miles east of Shiloh. Oh, I never *said* anything to her; I mean, about love or anything—you know. I wouldn't of. Have. But I day-dreamed. And mooned, and built magnificent castles. Especially in bed at night. My room then was directly over hers. It took very little imagination to envision a wilderness creature unburdened by the impedimenta of civilization, if you know what I mean. I did not sleep very restfully that September.

But by October, routines had been set up and the problems had diminished. I remember that I edged off washing my face so often and wearing a necktie to school. I rode my pony to school; Honeybee walked. Sometimes, not often, we walked together, but the enslavement had ended. My bloodstream had cooled, and I was being big-sistered not only by Opal but by Honeybee as well. She had been accustomed to brothers and knew how to handle them.

There was one embarrassing incident. Marvin Gaines, two years older than I, made a snickering off-color remark to her one day, in my hearing. I promptly kicked him in the rear. He turned, scowled, and ran at me. I dropped to the ground on all-fours and he tumbled ignominiously over me. Before he had gotten to his feet, Honeybee Phelps had hit him so hard with her fist that he must have been dazed.

"You come on home, Skeeter," she ordered, taking my hand.

Shucks. That unseated me from my big white charger; that took my suit of armor off. *Skeeter*! It relegated me to little-brother status. I remember sulking about it for several hours, but I got over that and Honeybee went blithely on with her assigned chores in our home, laughing and singing with Ellen, romping some and talking girl talk with Opal, and ignoring me altogether.

After supper that night I walked through the strawberry field and climbed the bobwire fence and went into the O'Reillys' yard. Mary-Margaret Sara and I did our higher arithmetic together, and her mother served us teacakes and milk.

It turned out that Honeybee and Aunt Rachel Harris had much in common. Both had been very backwoodsy in origin and rearing. Honeybee represented the daughter that Aunt Rachel never had. Both knew where to find wild greens for salads, down below the big, cool spring in our wooded area. Both knew where and how to gig bullfrogs to get their legs for food. They hunted down the great hollow trees that had bee honey in them, and got the honey without being stung, which was more than I ever learned to do. In autumn, they took me and other lads to pick wild muscadines—the most delicious "grapes" imaginable, each one a globule of nectar with a rubbery skin around it—and later on to gather wild haws. Both could catch fish, trap rabbits, and kill snakes without fear.

Honeybee would read books to Aunt Rachel and Uncle John, especially their Bible. Then the elders would interpret that gospel for her; and for me, if I was lucky enough to be a tagalong. All three of them could feed wild birds out of hand. All three of them felt that, if a hoot owl hooted outside your window after midnight, you would die before dawn unless you had put your shoes upside down under your bed. All three of them—and I, too, for months—put shoes upside down under our beds. Thus it was, quite incidentally, that the girl and the old folk enriched my boyish existence.

That about ends the saga of Honeybee Phelps, so far as I was personally concerned. I went on about my business, she about hers. The farm-ranch and the house were big; there was room for all of us, without impinging too much on each other. She stayed with us four years, until she eloped with a handsome rake named Fletcher Conway. I say rake—he wasn't all that bad. But he liked to do what the old folk called "sashay around too much," meaning, I'm sure, that he was simply charged with youthful energies, enthusiasms, and ambitions.

I do recall how hurt and disappointed Mama appeared to be over Honeybee's elopement. Mama predicted No Good End for any girl who would do such a thing. Papa took a more tolerant approach. He had found Honeybee, and I suspect that he had unconsciously responded to her femininity, her elemental charm, so that gallantry as well as open-house hospitality had been aroused in him. He told Mama it didn't follow that the young bride wouldn't make a good wife just because she had eloped.

But Mama knew. Honeybee had eloped from necessity. We did not discuss such matters in those years. The words *sex* and *pregnant* were never used, even in public print. But I can tell you, now, that Honeybee was "in a family way" and eloped when she and Fletcher discovered it.

No matter what Mama predicted, she was wrong. Honeybee's harum-scarum husband managed to get himself killed in an automobile accident. So there she was, all alone. Even then she did not go to the dogs, did not become a Fallen Woman or a public responsibility. She got herself a job teaching school in another town two hundred miles away, worked up to being principal, and altogether made such a fine career of it that there is a big new school named for her in that city today.

If Honeybee sinned, Papa at least did not judge her. He had opened his heart. He had opened his house. He was content with the ultimate outcome.

 # *Of Simple Kindness*

Nobody ever did tell me exactly how Papa found the second girl who came to live with us and get some schooling. It developed that he had plucked her out of some extremity of hopelessness far down in the sandy-land persimmon thickets of Rusk County, and we knew that his heart had been touched again.

Here I shall call her Helga Benstrom, although that was not her real name; also, I shall camouflage a few details that could identify her today.

My introduction to her came when Papa brought her to school one day and Superintendent Bittle called me into his office. He beamed broadly; but on seeing her and learning that she would live at my home, I was appalled. With a guest like that I would surely be ridiculed. Honeybee had been unprepossessing enough when she arrived that day in the rainstorm, but it soon developed that she enjoyed radiant health and spirit plus a remarkable amount of book learning. Now here stood an apparition of despair. Immediately I diagnosed Helga as consumptive. I wasn't at all sure what "consumption" was, except that it was some kind of physical horror that adults mentioned only in hushed tones, and which seemed to apply to people who bent over and looked sick. Helga was nearly six feet tall, or would have been if she hadn't let herself get so pitifully stooped.

My school behavior of late had not been above reproach, as Mr. Bittle well knew. Therefore, I felt that he was punishing me, having me escort this witch-like creature home. Absolutely no urge toward gallantry entered my mind. Mr. Bittle just edged both of us out of his office, and I started walking and Helga tagged along silently a few steps behind. I was sulking and glowering.

The silence became profound, except for the plop-plop-plop of her huge feet. I wore shoes today, but she did not, although the day was cold. I did not steer her along North High Street, where not only Mr. Bittle himself but also a lot of other high-class people lived. I led her straight on down to the grimy region of the railroad depot. There I suddenly saw a chance for respite.

A line of about twenty freight cars stood on a siding, leading northward toward my farm home. I clum up the steel-rod ladder of the first one—all right, then, *climbed*—got onto the little catwalk that formed a ridge for all such rolling stock, and just kept on walking. When I glanced down, Helga was plopping on the black cinders, then on the crossties that held the rails. As always, there were long rows of extra crossties in big square criss-cross stacks for curing, beside the main track. They really afforded wonderful places for kids to play. But I doubt if Helga ever had known what the word play meant.

We never said pea-turkey to each other all the way home (which is to say, we never spoke). When we finally entered the white-paling side gate to our yard, Mama was weeding her flower pots in the big pit we had dug for them. Strangely, she even had a four-o'clock in bloom in there, far out of season. You know what? Four o'clocks are pretty things any time and are a God's wonder, I vow. Usually grown in yards in summer, they have a rich green foliage sprinkled all over with gay red or yellow blossoms which—now get this—open *only* at four o'clock in the afternoon.

Well, Mama stood up, peered over her steel-rimmed glasses at us, then spoke. "Oren! And you must be Helga. Come in, honey, Mr. Arnold told me you'd be coming. Said he had taken you straight to school. How nice to see you." Mama put her arms around Helga and hugged her.

As Honeybee had done in her first moments with us, Helga burst into tears. Of letdown, I suppose; for surely she must have been what modern youths call uptight. And no doubt from homesickness. This was the first time, ever, that she had left her persimmon thicket, and

undoubtedly she was awed by our big white home. Actually, it was modest as "mansions" go; nevertheless, it must surely have been a dream palace with its white sculptured porch posts, bric-a-brac corner trim, and manicured lawn and hedges. I have since visited Longleat, the incredibly elaborate estate-home of the Marquis of Bath in England; also Chenonceaux and Amboise and Chaumont and other magnificent chateaus in France, and several great Italian villas, not to mention San Simeon in California and dozens of famous plantation homes in Dixie. But I am sure the impact of those places on me as an adult nowhere near matched that of our white farm home on Helga. She had a right to tremble and bawl, and Mama sensed her need.

There was no quick way to upgrade Helga and bring out a feminine sparkle, as there had been with Honeybee. This frustrated Mama and Ellen and Sis. They did do something about her appearance; her hair and her clothing. Beyond that, the situation was hopeless. Teeth protruded, in an era before orthodontia was even heard of there. Toes angled inward. The heavy stoop was rigid and the poor girl was sullen about any mention of it. In short, there was no sparkle, no personality, no charm. We also learned about her mentality. It was such that Professor Bittle had to edge the big girl into second grade, with kids less than half her age.

That, of course, made her a laughing stock at school. It also prompted Tunk Griffin to use his pocket knife and carve "Oren Loves Helga" on the slick bark of one of our sycamore trees at home. That in turn prompted me to sock Tunk on the ear—I missed his nose because he dodged—which was a mistake, because he then footballtackled me and he outweighed me by some forty pounds. But at the end of the hassle I was still ambulatory, so I went to our carpenter and blacksmith shop, got a wood rasp, and took that horrid statement off that tree. For one thing, I did not want Sarah to see it, in case that Dreamgirl of Perfection ever came to our farm. No, not Mary-Margaret Sara O'Reilly, the Catholic girl—that romance had cooled— but a seemingly much prettier Sarah with whom I was then secretly exchanging love notes, meeting surreptitiously at school, and rescuing from dragons in my dreams. But no male could dream about Helga. There, if ever, was a frump, a creature for us heartless ones to ridicule.

It is to my credit that I did no ridiculing; I just started pretending she did not exist. Mama, normally so outgoing, soon developed a reserve toward Helga. Often I caught her silently studying the girl and frowning, nonplussed. When Papa tried to be genial and hearty with her, she did not respond even to him. She seemed not to resent us, yet she showed no hint of understanding.

"Just let her be, Archie," Papa finally counseled Mama. "It'll take a while. Be nice to her. Oren, listen to me—you mind your own business, you hear? If I catch you pestering Helga——."

He did not finish his threat. He did not need to. Along with most people, I let Helga be.

She had come to us on a cold January day and my darker suspicions were aroused when she seemed to insist on going barefooted. Mama had to order the poor thing to wear stockings and shoes that had been given to her. She would show up in the milking pens in rainy, sleety, below-freezing weather, and be stripping old Jersey or old Muley before any of us saw her bare feet in the brownish manure slime.

"Oh, Helga girl, whatever do you mean?" Mama demanded that first time. "Do hurry in and wash your feet and put on warm shoes, honey, and the heavy stockings. Child, you will catch your death of pneumonia this way."

I doubt that she would have. Nature seems to take care of her own when they shrink back close to her bosom. Helga never caught even a cold—although today we know that a cold in the head has no relation whatsoever to low temperatures, but is caused only by contact with a vicious virus. Helga really seemed immune to everything.

"Will," I overheard Mama venture a firm diagnosis one day in March, "we have to face the fact that Helga is not like what we are. She is not—not mean or anything. But she is very dull. Even Professor Bittle said—well, as you know, he has pushed her away up into the tenth grade, so that she could be among children her own size, and the teachers just let her alone. But *he* knows, and they do too. Will, what are we going to do with her?"

"She is not a burden," Papa summed it up.

"No."

"And back at her home—Archie, they have nothing down there. Nothing!"

Mama's face showed distress. "The poor child is just *not right bright.*"

Mama's tone put that in italics. It was almost whispered, thereby emphasized. It was a good thing she had forgotten me or I should never have heard it, but I felt involved and worried, along with the parents. I, too, realized that Helga Benstrom was not right bright— another expressive idiom of the era. She never took part in any of our youth activities, such as hiking, or attacking the barn fort with corncobs, or playing circus. She would just stare whenever I flew my big kite, her mouth hanging open; wouldn't ever take the string or venture a comment. Once us kids got her into a game of "Drop the Handkerchief," and she couldn't understand what to do, not even when Alfred Rogers, a kindly soul, chose her for his girl and dropped it behind her in the circle. Embarrassed, we all just laughed self-consciously and pretended not to notice.

I do not recall that we East Texans had many mentally retarded folk. I can think of one or two Negroes who we felt were not altogether "there," but generally these were harmless and seemingly happy types, so nobody paid them much attention. In classroom during fifth grade a boy sort of acted crazy at times, and we learned that he had to be sent to an "institution." We kids had no idea what that was, nor cared much. It is easy to forget mentally handicapped associates if they are not your direct responsibility.

Helga was ours, so Papa and Mama faced up to it. They didn't have to; it was just the way they lived.

Uncle Johnny Barry was called into consultation about the matter. He expectorated (the word *spit* was considered inelegant) tobacco juice profusely—his sure sign of stress—then sat back to diagnose as best *he* could.

"It has been said," he spoke quietly, "that *everybody* can be smart if the desire to be so is felt."

Papa and Mama nodded. I nodded too; it seemed the proper response, even if I had little idea what Uncle Johnny was getting at. He went on.

"But I vow that is not so. I have studied the holy word. What was called demons—you remember about them—used to be in a few people. Nobody knew why. Today, we call those helpless ones crazy.

"I would say, that is a mistake. They are not crazy a-tall. There may be a few truly crazy people who have to be tied down at night or they do damage to themselves and others. Helga is no whit like that."

"Not a-tall," Papa agreed, while Mama and I nodded sagely again, and Ellen too, for she had now come into the family discussion.

"She is really a good girl," Mama allowed. "She causes no big trouble. Just—just can't seem to think."

"Yessum, po' chile," Ellen murmured.

"Yes, that's it," said Papa.

We had to let the matter go at that. An aura of gloom suffused our home for another week or two. We had failed, and my reaction was mainly one of helplessness and confusion.

Today I can look back on that moment in our family history only with a sense of regret. And yet, regret is the cancer of the mind. We were simply ignorant then, as ignorant in one sense as poor Helga herself.

In more recent years my wife Adele, as she neared grandmother age, became an expert in orthogenic teaching, meaning that she learned how to help mentally retarded children—those with low intelligence quotients who are sometimes called morons. She can testify that such luckless youths do not often suspect that they are ignorant; they assume themselves to be normal, then suffer acutely when forced into competition with children who really are.

So, as I look back now, I realize that Helga Benstrom was born sixty years too soon, because public awareness of mental retardation, mental illness, and such is relatively new. Only lately have we begun developing a sensible approach to it. I feel sure that Helga suffered mental illness on top of mental retardation (the two are not synonymous). Any of us, even the "smartest," the ones with the highest IQ, can become mentally ill. We may not even recognize the illness at first but, if it is ignored, the impact on ourselves and others may be profound. Those who love us most are likely to become confused, embarrassed, then horrified. It must have been that way with Helga's illiterate parents. I can well envision their appealing to Will Arnold in a sort of primitive desperation.

As recently as January, 1974, I interviewed a distinguished authority about all that. He is my friend, William Bede McGrath, M.D., Fellow of the American Psychiatric Association, and past president of a state psychiatric association. Dr. McGrath's comment is especially memorable, in view of what William Daniel Arnold and Archibald Laetitia Barry Arnold tried to do sixty years ago. In fact it is of tremendous importance to all of us in every walk of life today. This dedicated Christian psychiatrist said: "Eighty percent of all the mental illness that has ever come before me could have been prevented, or could yet be cured, *by simple kindness*!"

What a devastating commentary on our national mores, manners, and morals! But also, what a magnificent hope! *Simple kindness*!

There was no Adele Arnold to teach Helga; no Dr. McGrath with expert psychiatric counsel. However, there were Will and Archie Arnold and their black friend who loved them and, I think, loved all mankind, Ellen Austin, our cook.

"So she cain't learn nuthin' in school, you says, Mistuh Will." Big, fat Ellen was blinking her dark eyes, trying to think clearly that memorable evening. "But, suh, she a *sweet* chile. Maybe she don' need all that learnin' outen books." Ellen paused, still thinking. She would have called it "stud'n" about it. Mama and Papa remained silent, also thinking. Then Ellen resumed. And laid out a plan.

"You all let her leave school, suh. And ma'am. You take and let *me* learn that girl some things, sort of like. You knows me and my man George ain't got no chilluns a-tall our own selfs. That don't mean we ain't got no sense. I bet I could learn Miss Helga lots of good things to know. I got me some ideas, heah in mah min'." Ellen soberly touched her head.

I am happy to report that permission was granted. Also that Mama herself forgot about the majesty of book knowledge, formal schooling, and all that. "I can't read much, can't write at all," she spoke quietly about it, "and I get along fine." So, with Ellen, she pitched in to teach Helga from the persimmon thickets such things as the girl was capable of learning.

They were mostly physical. For example, at home she never had eaten or even heard of any kind of cornbread except the extremely heavy, "hard pone" composed only of cornmeal and a little salt mixed with water and fried in hog fat.

"Now, Helga, honey, you take and do it this way," Ellen coached, beaming and humming happily next morning. "You already got the meal in the pan. Now crack yo'self a egg into that. Heah, honey— knock de egg on de side of de pan, spread it open wif yo' finguhs and drop de insides all in, yaller and all. . . . Dat de way, dat jus' right! Now you takes some of dis good fresh cow milk and po' dat into de meal an' egg. . . . Good, good, you doin' fine, honey chile. Now put in a little salt. And me, I always adds a tablespoon of flour too, and a little bakin 'powduh. Dat keep de cornbread from bein' too crumbly, you unnerstan'?"

She showed Helga how to mix all that, not with any spoon and not —heavens to Betsy—with any modern, fancy electric blender gadget, which was unheard of then, and we had no electricity anyway. Mim- icking Ellen's big black hand, Helga smiled rather happily—a rare thing!—and swirled and beat the mixture with her own smaller white one.

"Like that?" the girl asked, absorbed now.

Ellen nodded. "You doin' it jus' right. I is proud of you, Helga, honey. Now just take dis pan and grease it with lard." Ellen showed her how. "Now po' de bread battuh in . . . slow . . . spread it aroun' wif yo' finguh . . . dat de way, dat's good! . . . Now, careful, open de oven do' and slide de pan in . . . Now close de do' . . . dat de way, you done it perfect!"

Ah me, enthusiasm; a contagious thing, always; an inspiration. That night at supper Ellen announced to all of us that the cornbread had been made entirely by her smart friend Helga, and didn't it smell good. It *did* smell good. It tasted even better, what with fresh turnip greens and salt sidemeat and buttermilk. Helga—po' chile—was in seventh heaven. I thought Mama was going to cry.

All right, that's the way they did it.

Mama moved into action with flowers, because Helga had already seemed intrigued with those in our pit and, later, those in the yard. She surely must have seen wild flowers, but she had no knowledge of domestic ones. Mama taught her about roses and violets and jonquils and those strange four o'clocks and geraniums and ferns and I don't remember what all, and Helga seemed like a normal person all the while, because here was something she could grasp. At long last

Mama and her guest had established rapport, a closeness, and both women obviously enjoyed it. I saw Papa slyly "studyin'" them one day, kneading his wad of chewing gum. He popped it back into his mouth and walked away, wearing an expression of content. Flowers were working magic—and don't they always? Some poet—I have no idea who, nor can I trace him—wrote this:

> Were I, O God, in churchless lands remaining
>   Far from all voice of teachers or divines
> My soul would find in flowers of thy ordaining
>   Priests, sermons, shrines!

They seemed to have precisely that effect on Helga.

The two women, black Ellen and white Archie, soon taught retarded Helga many other physical skills. How to wring a chicken's neck. (I know a modern bride from the city. Some countryman gave her a young rooster and told her to kill it by wringing its neck, then dress it out for supper. So she grasped it by the feet, swung it around her head a few minutes, and put it down! The poor rooster was shaken up a little, but it took to wing and nobody ever saw it again.) How to dunk the dead chicken in scalding water to loosen the feathers so they could be plucked easily. How to singe hairs off the carcass by twisting it in the flames of a lighted newspaper. How to gut it, saving the liver and gizzard. How to cut up the meat and bones. How to drop them in hot grease in the skillet.

Ellen had even explained the happy childhood ritual of the pulley-bone—wishbone, if you prefer. That night at table Helga somewhat shyly offered to pull with me. That was a major breakthrough. I felt elated, and I could see that the others at table did also. So I pulled, and tried to cheat, and lost. I wanted the short piece so that I could wish for a new saddle and get it. But, dang it all, I got the long piece and did get married before Helga did, I learned years later. And I never got that new saddle. I don't believe in pulleybones.

I need not go on. Surely I have made my point anyway; that mentally retarded people usually are educable to some degree. If you have the patience to teach them; the desire, the inborn goodness of heart.

In about a year Helga asked to go back home and "help her mama and papa and little sisters." She knew so much, now, that she felt a strong urge to—what? Show off? Yes, likely. And to share? Yes, surely! From my folks she had learned that priceless skill also.

Outfitted with a new hair-do, new clothing, a wholly new brightness in her eyes, and a potential that she could never have hoped to find in the deep persimmon thicket, she was taken back to her unpainted shack of a home.

One more detail here.

That same distinguished modern psychiatrist, Dr. Bill McGrath, has one other inspiriting piece of new knowledge that I yearn to share with you. Highly apropos, it comes from his own new book, *Mental Fitness*. On page 104 he says:

Altruism, the instinct to sacrifice, is the least understood and still the most powerful of all the instincts. Given an invitation, it will supersede selfishness and sex. It will almost always supplant competitiveness and cruelty. To issue the invitation and to create conditions in which the individual can experience the thrilling goodness of sacrifice—that will require our most thoughtful concern.

Just think a moment! Simple kindness, to prevent or cure mental illness. Altruism, the strongest urge, which could bring about the dreamed-of millenium in human relations!

I will now let you decide how skillfully Will Arnold and Archie Arnold and Ellen Austin, who never even heard of the word psychiatry, applied those two marvelous concepts.

 *A Singular Strength*

Not all of the elder Arnolds' open-heart efforts were so touchingly successful as were those involving Helga and Honeybee. There were country boys who came to us too, and the record on some of them changes the mood. No special dramas attended their arrival. The news simply had got around that the Arnolds in Henderson sometimes took in needy youths to help them get an education; hence a despairing, or even merely an aspiring, father might come to Mr. Will with his hopes showing.

In our rural regions the need for any help was great. Modern youths, accustomed to fine yellow school buses, elaborate schoolroom equipment, highly trained teachers, and such cannot begin to envision the lack of opportunities back there in post-Civil War America, especially in the South. Not until after World War I did any important upgrading begin. But somehow that deprivation begat a singular strength, a mental toughness that has paid off.

None of the boys came from families as poor as those of the girls. Young Otho Davis, for example, arrived at our home well dressed. He even had a necktie on. He wore a clean new hat. Going around hatless in those years would have tagged a young man as slightly "tetched." Otho also wore a "nice" suit that must have cost all of ten or twelve dollars. He had on shined shoes over nonsmelling socks. I remember taking him, with some pride, up town to Benson Alford's home to see the first automobile owned in Henderson. Mr. E. B. Alford himself, Benson's father, came out to demonstrate the miracle for us. He managed to back it into the buggy shed that housed it. Damage to the shed and car exceeded one hundred dollars. America's automotive era had begun!

Otho already knew to say "Yes, sir" and "Yes, ma'am" and "please" and "thank you" and "Let me do that for you, Miss Archie" and "Mr. Will, you just sit down, sir, and I will feed the stock." But he also was not above tousling my mop of black-Irish hair and saying, "Oren, you come on and help me carry in the stovewood." Darn him. We had two empty piano boxes for wood, one behind the great kitchen range, another in the hall for fireplaces and iron heaters, and by some strange magic they were eternally empty. And yet I enjoyed being big-brothered by Otho. He knowed—knew—so much more'n me. Also I soon learned that no bigger boy dared jump on me as long as Otho was around. He was strong.

I will not belabor the record of Otho Davis. Space here simply does not permit a detailed delineation of all the nice things I could say about him, including the fact that he was firm-jawed handsome, as the girls of Henderson quickly realized. Would you want to pay maybe three dollars more for a book just to hear me brag on my boyhood friend Otho? No.

He went on through school, creating no particular excitement. I am sure that Mama and Papa regarded him with pride and joy. When he left, he planned to go on to college somewhere; then I lost track of him for years. But when, as a young married man myself, I came back to visit Henderson, people told me that, yes, Otho Davis sure had done well. Seems he married a pretty girl, had a good family going, owned a lot of land, had good crops, made good money in feeder cattle, was a good citizen in every sense—and how are *you* getting along, Oren? I was bored hearing that word "good" when people spoke of Otho. I do not know if he is still alive. I hope he is and that he reads this. His time in our home, though somewhat colorless in retrospect, due perhaps to his "goodness," was one of the happiest fruits of my parents' open-hearted hospitality and love.

Draper was next. Draper Taliaferro.

I have little to report on that young gentleman, though I remember him well indeed. As I meditate on his personality and character, only one descriptive word comes to mind—colorless. Some people, especially the good ones, are like that, you know.

He, too, was what Mama and Papa naturally termed a "good" boy, which itself was enough to make him a nonentity among his contemporaries. Whoever wants to be known as "good" in his teen years? Drape—we shortened his name to that—did everything he was told to do, and little else. He was nowhere near the take-charge fellow that Otho was. Oh, yes, he studied his lessons. He helped on the farm. He learned to dehorn yearling bulls, which is valuable knowledge in Texas. He could sharpen hoes by upending them and kneeing their handles firmly to hold them against a post, then filing the blade and not cutting the heel of his thumb. That took some doing; ask any farm boy. On winter nights he stayed mostly in his room; he did not come down to share in our family fellowship unless Mama specifically ordered him to. Even then, he had little to say. There was a small wood-burning heater up there in his room, but the fire in it would of course die down. And because his was an attic room, right against the shingles, winter would sneak its sleety fingers in there and build half an inch of ice in your water glass, cracking it. Therefore, Mama, mothering this forlorn lad, would heat one of her heavy flatirons in our fireplace downstairs, wrap it in a newspaper and a piece of old quilt, and let Drape take it upstairs to bed with him, pampering him exactly as she did me. Well, that was Mama for you. But if Drape ever said "thank you" I never heard him. Then, as now, youth tended to take handed-out luxuries for granted.

All that year he was with us I had little to do with Drape. Not that we avoided each other, but we simply had divergent interests. I had learned to trot downtown and spend a whole dime attending the open-air "moom pitcher" show every Saturday night, because that gloriously curvaceous maiden-in-distress, Miss Pearl White, was on the screen in *The Perils of Pauline.* Apparently Drape was about as romantic and imaginative as a bucket of mud. He stayed home, and I never knew what he done there on those Saturday evenings that were so happy for me. Did there, I mean; Sis would chide me to this day, if I didn't make it clear that I really *know* better grammar.

Very well, then. Drape got some Town school learnin', his papa came in a buggy, they shook hands with all of us, and disappeared down our front lawn and on down that road paralleling the railroad track. In three or four hours, no doubt, they were back home in the distant wilderness. I never heard what happened to Drape. Probably nothing. When some people hear opportunity knock, they open the door, then coast; they are not destined to make anything happen. At the moment back there, I couldn't care less. Come to think of it, I don't even care now. The Drapers of earth make no impact.

But a slightly older lad whom I am calling DeWitt—now there was a cat of a different color!

Drape had been a loner; not malicious, not stupid, but just introverted, glum, and unattractive, so that nobody really wanted to fraternize with him. But seemingly everybody could fraternize with De-Witt, an extrovert if ever there was one.

You know the type. He seems to be universal, more common here in the 1970's than ever. He can be any age from twelve on up, but his most marked impact today is as an upper-teen boy, when he is brash to a fault, yet somehow engaging. He swaggers a little; roars around outrageously on a motorcycle. Or he guns his hopped-up old bomb of a car to a stoplight, then sits there and makes it sound VROOOO-O-O-OOM, VROOOO-O-O-OOM, by dancing on the accelerator and wasting gas for which his pappy pays. DeWitt would have loved doing all that.

His apparent wildness set Uncle Johnny to worrying from the very start. So Uncle Johnny took it upon himself to invite DeWitt to attend church with the family, maybe even Sunday school as well.

"Aw naw, not me," DeWitt grinned in his superior, all-knowing manner. "I don't believe in all that stuff."

Such heresy! I fully expected a bolt of lightning to zigzag down right that moment, even though the sky was crystal turquoise, and strike DeWitt dead on the spot. I sort of even hoped it would.

It didn't. And wise old Uncle Johnny did not panic. He expectorated profusely, wasting a fresh cud of tobacco; harrumphed; adjusted his chair there on his corner of the back porch and in effect pronounced judgment.

"Anybody," he began, "who says he is an atheist is showing the greatest possible conceit. He is saying that he is smarter than ninety-nine percent of all the kings and queens and presidents, than all the great philosophers, statesmen, scientists, artists, authors, industrialists, lawyers, farmers, doctors, ranchers, housewives; in fact, might nigh everybody on earth. If there is no God, then the whole of life is point-less!" He was revved up.

That trenchant summary sort of cooled DeWitt. His mind could not cope with such profound reasoning, any more than shallow or im-mature minds can today, whatever their age. He just kept on forcing a silly grin. Finally he edged away and Uncle Johnny let him be.

In another and more down-to-earth sense, the boy had come to our home already "educated." Which is to say, he knew how to shoot craps. I had never even heard of the game, naïve young skeeter that I was. Oh, I *thought* I was worldly wise; today we would call it sophisticated. But today I also know that "sophistication" is America's grand social delusion. As generally used, the word is close akin to sophistry, or false reasoning, and to the immature manifestations of many sophomores such as the modern campus "streakers."

DeWitt was a "swinger" sixty years before that slang term entered the language. First proof was when I caught him shooting craps with a Negro man unknown to me, and apparently winning. I say "caught" —I did not tattle on him, not, in fact, being sure that any sin or misbehavior was involved; so why mention it to Papa? I just did not know about dice. No dice had ever been seen in our home; and, if it comes to that, no playing cards. So I merely shrugged off the matter of the crap game behind the smokehouse and went on about my business. But my curiosity gradually swelled, so that later I asked my friend George Austin about those dice. Just to make myself clear, I explained casually what I had seen.

"Sho nuff?" he seemed horrified at the news. "What nigguh was throwin' dices with Mistuh DeWitt?"

That worried me. George was not funning. But I had to answer so I said, "The one with the knife scar on his neck."

"Chatman! That stinkuh! Dog bite his black hide, I puts a knife *thu'* his neck! Learnin' my white folks how to gamble!"

George stalked off grumbling, saddled a horse, and galloped away toward our nearby Negro colony. I longed to follow but something —call it wisdom—told me to stay home and keep quiet. Then that night our telephone rang. When I answered it, Sheriff Joel Hale asked for Papa, who was out.

"All right then, Oren, you go find him and tell him I had to arrest his man George. He's in jail here. Beat up another black man. George has cooled off now and I will let him go. But you tell your pappy to talk to George."

Phooey. I never told Papa nuthin'. And I told George I wouldn't tell Papa. George's face lit up like one of them new-fangled 'lectric light globes, which many of the town people already had, a few even in their homes, as well as their stores. George put a massive black arm around my neck and grabbed its wrist with his other hand and pretended to squeeze hard, his way of expressing exuberance.

"I sho' 'preeshy-izes that, Skeeter man. You my frien'. Anytime *you* need help, I'm heah." But I already knew that.

"Did you stab his neck like you said?"

"Me? Naw, naw, Skeet. You knows me—I ain't mean. All I done was ram my fis' down his th'oat thu' his big mouf—WHOO!" George broke into laughter. "But he won't mess around Mistuh DeWitt shootin' dices no mo'."

So nothing of real importance resulted from that facet of DeWitt's education; truth is, Chatman learned more than DeWitt. But very soon another episode shaped up and it touched all our lives. It began in what we called the cotton room or cotton house, although it was really a part of our barn complex. A big operation like our farm and ranch business required not one but four main "barns" plus two smaller structures, the latter including a blacksmith-carpenter shop and a house for canning such produce as peaches, tomatoes, and corn. All those in addition to Mama's two chicken houses, and several large coops. Actually, it looked like a village, out there behind our main house.

That cotton house was used at times to store the fleecy raw fiber until we had time to take it to the gin. Enough to make four or five bales could be piled up in there, like snowdrifts in a mountain world. A place to play? It probably was the grandest one in Henderson. Who needed a thousand dollars' worth of store-boughten, factory-made junk toys such as complicate the lives of city kids today? Not us! I doubt if I received fifty dollars' worth of store toys in all my boyhood; all I remember now is a two-dollar Daisy air rifle and a little red wagon. But we made jillions of things, my friends and I did, in our carpenter shop, with guidance from Papa and Uncle Johnny and Tip and Buck at times, but mostly from our own ingenuity. We had us a flyin' jenny (merry-go-round) big enough to ride on, and a Ferris wheel that could carry eight kids up and around thrillingly, and somewhat dangerously, plus an endless stream of swings and trapezes and tight wires to walk as in the circuses, all that. But the cotton house—

hoo boy! What hilarious jumping, tumbling, wrastlin', shouting, whooping, laughing excitement *that* place afforded!

Mama had sent me out there to hunt for hidden hen nests, as per routine. No guests were around, no play under way, so far as I knew.

But as I approached that room with strands of cotton poking out through its cracks, I did hear a sort of subdued laughing-moaning concerto in there. The strange duet tones arrested me. Those definitely were juvenile voices and one was female. I couldn't quite distinguish the words, so I edged up close and put my eye near one of the cracks in the weathered planks.

Sure enough, there they were. DeWitt, our white-boy guest, supposedly come to town to get an education, and slightly older black Leonie Jenkins, furthering that education.

I am not now just sure how old I was. In fact, throughout this book I have not worried about chronology, but have allowed flashbacks and overlappings in time, as convenience seemed to demand. But at that moment I must have been somewhere around thirteen, and I guarantee you I already "knew all about sex."

No, not from experience. And no, absolutely no parent or other authorized person had ever told me anything at all about it. Such wasn't done in those years. Any child was supposed to learn the Facts of Life on his own, somehow. That usually meant bits at a time in snickering conversations in or near outhouses, mostly at school, where our long privy was two hundred yards down a hill and shockingly devoid of sanitation. I had one great advantage over city boys; I was living on a farm. You cannot watch a rooster chase a hen, help Papa breed a stallion to a mare, behold the rumblings and pawings of a bull preliminary to his mounting a heifer, without acquiring some truly scientific facts. From such combined sources I not only knew that intercourse caused human babies, but I also understood clearly that people often engaged in it purely for pleasure.

DeWitt and Leonie obviously were engaged in it for pleasure. But I shall not detail what I saw during the twenty minutes or so that I stood spellbound with my eye plastered against that crack in the planks. The literary world of today already has a plague of pornography, because a lot of stupid authors flaunt it for money, which is simply a low form of pimping.

Yet I felt such unctuous indignation—or maybe it wasn't so unctuous—that later in the day I decided I had to challenge DeWitt with
what I had observed.

"I seen what you and Leonie done," I spoke frankly, scowling,
standing spread-legged, thumbs hooked in the belt of my knicker-
bocker pants. We were there in the barnyard.

I was smaller than DeWitt. But also I was more swift on my feet;
besides which, something told me that I had him on the defensive. He
had broken a Commandment. He had "insulted" one of our own
Negro girls, who lived in one of the small rent houses on our farm,
and often helped us chop cotton in spring and pick it in fall.

DeWitt blanched. He looked off, looked back at me, bit his lower
lip, walked away. Sex! Unspeakably sinful any time if illicit, even
with a white girl. But with a *black* girl—O God! The sky would fall
and we both knew it.

I watched him slink out of sight around the smokehouse while I
stood there trying to think what I ought to do next. So for a few hours
I just bided my time, but I was miserable.

That night DeWitt slyly packed his few things and, unseen, left
us forever, trudging eleven miles on back to his rural Rusk County
village, we later learned.

When Papa finally got around to asking me if I had any idea why
he ran away, I up and told on DeWitt. I mean, well, it was my home,
my barn and cotton room, even one of my Negro friends if it got to
that, for I had chopped and picked in the same group of "hands"
with Leonie Jenkins many a time. Papa sensed that attitude in me and
honored it.

"Just as well he left, I guess," he ruled calmly. "We can't have that
sort of thing around here, can we?"

"No, sir," I agreed, man to man.

I cannot now say that we handled the matter in the best possible
way. I can only report what we did. And report further that, nine
months later, Leonie died in childbirth. She was about seventeen. And
yes, she was a pretty thing. When I see Leslie Uggams on television
today, I am seeing Leonie's face in my mind's eye. In retrospect I do
not entirely blame DeWitt; nor Leonie. The sex urge in adolescents is
a powerful and dangerous force not to be laughed off or at. I am sure

that DeWitt was *driven*; quite beyond his control. Leonie would have been similarly driven, also highly flattered by such attention from a white boy. Caution? Discretion? Whoever can summon that when vibrant lifeblood is racing through your veins?

Leonie's parents grieved dramatically and audibly for a week, the mother walking up and down the lane to our house crying and shrieking and lifting her arms and calling on the Lord, so that not even my Mama could comfort her. The girl's father, we were told, sat and brooded. Then next Sunday afternoon a barefoot black man ran panting up to our kitchen door and called for my Papa.

"Mistuh Will, suh," reported he with obvious agitation. "Miss Leonie's pappy, he mean drunk, and he goin' around eve'ywhere totin' a big ol' pistol sayin' he gonna kill you!"

Papa did not panic; he was never very demonstrative. "Why me?" he asked calmly. "What have I done to him?"

"He say you to blame, Miss Leonie die. He say it yo' fault 'cause you brung that DeWitt boy here to yo' farm and let him see Leonie. He mean it, Mistuh Will, suh! He will sholy try to shoot you down!"

"Well, thank you," Papa nodded. "I will look into it."

Look into it? How?

What does one man do when he learns that another is out to shoot him? Get his own gun, skulk around so as to shoot first? Run? Hide? Papa should, of course, have called his friend Sheriff Hale and let that official handle the matter. Papa did no such thing.

"Maybe I *was* partly to blame," he muttered, within my hearing but unaware of my presence. He often talked to himself when agitated, as many people do. "I should have watched him closer."

He stalked off across our strawberry field, unarmed, toward the Negro colony, after ordering the rest of us to stay home. So I never saw the finale, but George Austin did and proudly told us about it later.

Sure enough, Papa found the miserable, distraught and drunken man, and sure enough he was carrying a huge loaded pistol ready for instant use. Papa first saw him from a distance of some fifty yards, but kept on walking steadily toward him.

The Negro stood there glaring. In one second, murder could have been done. But the Negro made no move. Papa never lost stride until he stopped an arm's length from the man. Then he quietly reached over, took the pistol from him without resistance, and stuck it into his own belt.

"Now go on home, Jenkins," Papa ordered calmly. "You need to go to bed and rest, so you can think. Everything is all right now. Just turn around and go home, and I will do the same."

Papa walked the half mile back to our house slowly, climbed our porch steps without saying a word to any of us, and went on along the porch to the big double doors that led into our central hallway. Over those doors, in front of the big double transom up there, was a sort of ledge or shelf about a foot wide. Papa reached high and placed the old hogleg-type pistol up there while we silently watched. Still saying absolutely nothing, he then moved to his cot on the porch, lay down, and went to sleep.

No mention was ever made of the episode. That gun rested up there four years, untouched, until one day in Papa's absence my oldest brother, Tip Arnold, took it down, carried it back to Jenkins, and returned it to him without comment.

Hospitality? Papa's "open heart"—I have been pleased to call it that here—over the years was not all sweetness and light, not always manifest in simple and easy ways. Frequently, in any strong person's life, one of the major components of kindness is courage.

We never knew what life made of DeWitt; or what he made of life. Perhaps he had acquired at least some bit of upgrading from his stay with us. It is possible that he is still alive and will read this with —what? Astonishment? Shock? A surge of nostalgia, of wishing for a rerun on his youth so that he might improve it? All of us have such moments at times. Surely he will be curious to know about his illegitimate son.

It is a pleasure to report that the baby, under loving care, grew up in his grandparents' home to be a handsome fellow. About thirty-five years after his birth I managed a good visit with him one day in Houston. He was married, well respected, happy in a good-paying city job. So far as I could learn, the events surrounding his appearance on earth had all been forgotten. Life marches on.

 *The Forward Look*

One other boy came to Henderson to live with us, and was so extraordinary as to merit special attention here.

He came from what might be called the extremes of rural environment. It is difficult for modern dwellers in chromium-trimmed, high-rise condominium apartments to envision an East Texas "country" setting as of 1915 or so. Aboriginal is an apt term for the area from which this boy arose. There were a few farms, a few unsightly villages, and not much else. (American villages generally have always lacked the picturesque beauty and charm of European villages, and that is a pity.) Almost no house was painted. Fences were saggy makeshifts of split rails or loose barbed wire. Livestock was unpedigreed and inefficient, and so, too, were most of the people.

And yet, incredibly, our boy came to us "educated" in a remarkable way. Some rich inheritance had enabled him to respond to the beauty, the wonder, in vast primeval forests of hickory and oak and pine, of wild cherry and black haw, of redbuds and the shy, seemingly virginal dogwood blossoms. "Dogwood" is a poor folk name for that wonderful tree, and our new boy taught me its inspiring legend.

It had furnished wood for the Cross, said he with proper awe. Because of that, Jesus gave it gorgeous white blossoms in the shape of a cross, two long and two short petals, in their center a crown of thorns, and nail prints on the outer edges of the petals, brown with rust and stained with red, so that all who see them will remember.

Endless other wild flowers adorned the woodlands and fields, and still do. Motion and sound came from the mocking birds, the bob whites, the redbirds, bluebirds and jays, the wild foxes, rabbits, deer, opossums, raccoons, and many another wilding. But for the people, any contact with the outside world was a rarity. Even the RFD mail carrier had little to carry, in or out. Town folk—"social workers," forsooth!—felt that such an area was stifling for all human beings.

Not so for Jon Demosthenes Blaine.

He came to us fully endowed. For instance, could any boy, anywhere, have a more aristocratic name?

I hold no brief for the preposterous guff called "astrology," but as a fun-superstition we early-twentieth-century Texans often said that so-and-so seemed to have been born under a lucky star. Furthermore, fate often seems to have something superior in mind for the Jons or Johns of this world. As a name it is comparable in popularity to the matchless Mary, and I have never known a John who was not honorable in at least some degree. It was so with our Jon. From the very beginning, his manner and manners displayed the rare charisma, the mystique.

The mental picture of him comes into sharpness now as I envision him on that first day with us back there in the slow-paced years. The setting was in the quarter-acre fenced corral behind our main barn, with its four big, wide feed troughs for horses and mules, and wild birds that eternally fluttered there as freeloaders. I clum—climbed— the heavy plank fence right after school that day, then paused up on the top plank, surprised.

Here was a stranger shucking corn for the stock, ear by ear from a bushel basket, at one of those big feed troughs. He was doing it with obvious speed and skill and, as he worked, he whistled. It seemed to be a sort of operatic concerto, not just idle sound; rapid scales shooting up high in tremolo effects, then ranging to deep bass. His back was toward me so he hadn't spotted me yet. I watched him blend the rhythm of the song into the motions of corn shucking, swaying a little with it, working fast and obviously enjoying life. Almost instantly there he became the boy I yearned to be.

Nobody had to tell me that Papa had found us another guest; by now I was used to that as routine. I did not care how Jon came to us. I only knew that there stood a Personality. One who could in effect make us forget the Drapers and DeWitts and the Helgas and even the Othos and the Honeybees.

Him and me—all right, he and I—managed to get acquainted right there; rather awkwardly, on my part. I think he set my inferiority complex ticking—which never has been real easy to do, I might add. I am opposed to inferiority complexes; if you must feel some sort of silly complex, then make it a superior one. But for a few moments there I almost wanted to call Jon "Mister." His quick, open smile soon scotched that impulse, and we were buddies before I realized it.

Big George Austin was there also that late afternoon, doing end-of-day chores. So me and my new friend Jon shucked corn together and I toted the baskets of shucks across the lot and into the cowpens, because cows love them and horses don't. Then I throwed six bales of hay down from the high barn loft and Jon busted them open and swished the three tie wires from each bale up onto the low barn roof, where a pile of them already was rusting and waiting for anybody who ever needed a piece of wire. Him and me took the tightly pressed "blocks" of field hay to the slatted racks above the corn troughs, shook them loose, and threwed the fragrant stuff up and in, smelling the goodness of it, laughing a little the while. Togetherness! Enjoyable! Our stock would greedily eat the flinty corn first, then more leisurely munch their dessert, the cured hay, until around midnight or so, after which they would go to sleep.

All this while, big George shoveled up the green manure from that morning, then greased our wagons for tomorrow's use. As Jon had whistled his operatic aria (I never knew where he learned it) George hummed-sang his beloved *The little boy Jesus say to me, Come set heah under this big tree. . . .*

Jon never tired. Never! You couldn't *work* him down. Not that anybody tried, except himself. Energy. It is a nebulous thing at best. An intangible. An unpredictable "something" as impossible to define as is electricity, which itself is energy. I think maybe it really develops physiologically and psychologically combined, in what we call the whole man or woman; the mature minded ones, the gifted few who stride ahead under all circumstances, adverse or good. Jon was like that. There seemed to be nothing about our complex farm and ranch enterprise that he couldn't do and enjoy doing.

I remember one afternoon after school when he, single-handed, re-shingled our cow feed house. Nobody had told him to; he had simply noticed that the old pine shingles up there were curling and splitting and would soon be letting rain water in to sour the rich, yellow cottonseed meal, which we put on the cottonseed hulls for our milk cows, and which they so loved.

Mama soon loved Jon like a son. She often gazed at him a bit wistfully, and I am sure she was wishing I might turn out like that as I grew along. She made me take to wearing a dang old necktie to school, just because he did so voluntarily. But then, maybe that was why the luscious Sarah fell in love with me that year. Or said she did, in assorted notes passed along. Ah me, the poignancy of *that* experience. When I dared confide to Jon about it, he dismissed it too casually, saying, "It will pass." Impossible! For a day or two there, I hated him.

Papa seemed more man-to-man with Jon. When they talked, I felt that it was much like Papa's visiting with Colonel Bob Milner, who had been President of A. and M. College. They seemed never to limit themselves to such inane topics as the likelihood of rain and the baseball game at school come Friday and the latest joke about the horseless carriage. They talked more about what the Texas Legislature was doing, even what Congress and the President, away off in Washington, were doing; and Mister Will, sir, don't you think if we terraced all your sloping land it would stop that costly erosion?

I had no idea what erosion was. But apparently Papa did.

"I expect you are right, son." He called all boys son, if he liked them. "We've sure had some gullywashers."

"You want me to look into it, sir? Cotton'll soon be all picked. And the corn pulled, the fodder gathered, bundled and hauled in. The stock can graze there a month to eat up all the rich speckled peas and vines you planted as ground cover, also some of the corn stalks themselves—they have sugar in them, which is nourishment. After that, Mr. Will, we could run the stalk cutters on both cotton and corn, and put the erosion-control terraces in while other work is slack. But first we'd have to get the land surveyed. So we would know how to curve the terrace dams."

Papa looked at the young fellow with obvious astonishment. "How is it you know so much, Jon? I happen to know you was born a country hick, like I myself was."

Jon's engaging smile flashed, even as he blushed in modesty. "But sir, you didn't *grow up* a country hick! Not in your mind. I have never known a smarter man than you." Jon belonged in the diplomatic corps.

"Hah! In book learnin' I scarcely know north from east. Whereas you———." he looked down at the boy.

"Abraham Lincoln was a country hick, sir."

"That damnyankee!" Papa grinned. "But old Abe was all right, I don't misdoubt. Meant well. And yes, I see what you mean. Taught himself, yes, right there in his own backwoods. Born low, but wouldn't stay low. I respect that. You got holt of some good books down where you lived, like Abe did? Talked with any smart people wherever you could?"

Jon nodded. "Yes, sir. About the terracing—I had long visits with some road and tract surveyors who spent time in our area. Also I borrowed a lot of books about Texas botany and zoology. Then I———."

Papa interrupted. "What's them?"

"Plant and animal life, sir. But it was those government surveyors who told me all about terracing to control erosion."

Papa, no less than I, was listening closely. "Be dogged," said he, taking his chewing gum out to knead it in thought. "Yes, Jon. Terracing. It's what Bob Milner's been saying. But he, uh, has not pressed the matter, because he knows the surveying will cost money. Maybe some year when I can afford it, I can hire———."

"Excuse me, sir, but *I* can do it. You can rent me a transit for almost nothing. And I know how to run simple surveys like that."

Transit. I'm sure Papa knew what that was, but I didn't, and I felt left out. Sometimes it was—is—hellish to be too young.

"You just lend me Oren to help with the stakes and things, and hold the marker while I sight through the telescope. We'll need a buckboard to haul everything around. How about it, sir?"

Papa turned and put an arm around him. "Be dogged!" said he again. "You go to it, son! And learn Oren how, hear? I'll pay you both a wage." Which made my spirits soar again.

So then, come planting time for cotton, corn, peas, melons, and other stuff next spring, our loamy plowed-and-harrowed fields were indeed graced by long low flat dams curling against the normal water wash, pooling the rainfall rather than allowing gullycutting to destroy tenderling plants and leach priceless minerals away. We lost no tillable space at all, because crop rows could be planted at their usual spacing right along the broad tops of those dams.

Colonel Milner got wind of it and came out to see. He went back to his newspaper and his telephone and drummed a big meeting right on our farm fields. Nearly three hundred farmers from all over Rusk County gathered there. The colonel also brought in two experts on agronomy—which word he had to define for Papa and me—from A. and M., and a lot of coffee drinking and speech-making and hand-shaking and I-just-do-declaring was done. Papa was written up in the paper as a forward-thinking man of the soil, which same he truly was. Next time he ran for office of tax assessor he got seven times as many votes as his opponent did. But then, the opponent was a younger man from Town whose own father had allegedly been a Republican, poor soul.

Papa *tried* to give proper credit to Jon Demosthenes Blaine. The paper did mention him as the surveyor. But he was too young for many of the old hard-bitten farmers to take him seriously. They had sons older'n him at home.

But Uncle Johnny knew.

Uncle Johnny was no fool, as I have repeatedly emphasized. He was present during all that development of the terraces. Matter of fact, we learned too late that he himself knew how to handle simple surveying. It just hadn't occurred to him that it could be used to terrace land. Anyway, he was too kindly to butt in on Jon Demosthenes (Uncle Johnny always called him by both given names).

But those achievements by Jon pointed up the boy's value to all of us. It was our cook, Ellen Austin, who, shrewd woman that she was, first put the matter into proper perspective.

"We-all brung Mistuh Jon 'moss-en-nees up heah to give him some learnin' and he'p him improve hisself. But truf is, we gittin' mo' learnin' from him than he gittin' from us, seem like."

Everybody laughed, Jon included, there in our gathering on the porch by the water well. He tried to deny the honor, turning it off as merely Ellen's nice joke.

But Papa nodded agreement with Ellen, and Mama said, "That's so, Ellen." And Uncle Johnny said, "I don't misdoubt but what Jon Demosthenes was *sent* to us." We all understood what he meant; Uncle Johnny nearly always turned any good news into a blessing direct from God.

As a matter of fact, John Barry and Jon Blaine had already established intellectual rapport. In the subsequent family talk, Uncle Johnny explained that if your brain is so arranged, I mean if you are just naturally a gifted person anyway, you can acquire and retain high-level knowledge anywhere. Certainly a pristine wilderness such as Jon's homeland would encourage much learning—how about Henry Thoreau and John Muir and even Johnny Appleseed—two more Johns! *They* did all right, living and learning and loving among the trees, ponds, streams, flowers, wild beasties, and open skies.

It was young Jon Demosthenes Blaine who gave our family what I now think of as The Forward Look. For instance, at one family gathering Jon declared that the new horseless carriage would surely revolutionize human society.

"How can it?" Uncle Johnny challenged, though I think he agreed.

"Well, sir, the stagecoach has been replaced by the train. But the train must have a costly track, and will therefore be replaced by the motor car which can go right to your door. And in fifty years it will have enabled all the American people to swap their knowledge, on all kinds of subjects. The more knowledge that comes, the more civilization advances."

"Be dogged!" murmured Papa.

"The aeroplane now," Jon was gazing afar, speaking humbly. "Some men named Wright got into a box-like contraption with an engine and made it fly! Others have flown similar contraptions since then. In time, we will all be flying; maybe even as far as from here in Henderson to Dallas. Won't need a railroad train, or even a motor car."

But that of course was brash youth speaking, and everybody else smiled knowingly, tolerantly. In my citified wisdom I felt called upon to put in a put-down. So I smirked a little and pontificated: "We got about as much chance of flyin' from here to Dallas as we have of walking on the moon." Which I felt was brilliant.

Uncle Johnny evidently did not. He expectorated tobacco juice, peered over his spectacles at Jon and said, "Please continue."

"Today people on ships can touch telegraph keys and send out dot-dash messsages to other ships and to shore, right through the air with no wires at all. We have read how the *Titanic* called for help by wireless, and did thereby save at least a few people from drowning."

"Yes," Papa nodded. "That's so."

It went on in that vein until I grew tired of seeing Jon gather so much adulation. Who was he, an outsider, to be so much smarter'n me?

Well, he was a guy who was much smarter'n me, that's who. And try as I would, I could not make myself hate or even dislike him. All of us continued to pick his brain whenever we could. Once it was when him and me—he and I—sat and rested from picking strawberries, eating too many big luscious red ripe ones. Our backs were "broken" from stooping, and our knees were sore from crawling along the beautiful rows. Why didn't God put strawberries—queen of all fruits, next to a tree-ripened peach—on bushes about waist high, like He did blackberries?

So Jon expanded his theme, about grandeurs in the future. He told us in effect that "we ain't seen nuthin' yet," and that man can hardly even envision the great things to come in science and other areas of knowledge. The ideas that he planted continued to haunt me as I plodded through my teen years.

Jon Demosthenes eventually moved on, as all our other young guests had. He made his way through college and became an educator—which was not surprising. Last I heard tell of him he was still being honored for that Forward Look, and was lecturing not only in his own college as a professor, but, as a guest, in others as well. For all I know he may still be teaching somewhere, somehow. He couldn't be more than eighty years of age, and that isn't "old"; it is just fully matured. If you happen to read this, Jon—God bless you, man! And thank you for being my boyhood friend.

"Yes, suh," Ellen Austin reminded all of us again one day soon after Jon left our home, "he come heah to git a heap o' learnin' from us, and I says he give us mo' than we give him."

But isn't that the usual, divine result of open-heart sharing?

 *Twigs from the Tree*

Up to this point I have proclaimed the goodness, the kindness and generosity, of two parents and an uncle. Now what about the next generation? Five children of Will and Archie Arnold were at home in the big white house on the hill that was perpetually "open." So what attitudes did they develop?

One fact has come through sharply clear—heredity is a powerful factor, more powerful than any environment. Scientists today know that our lives are controlled mainly by chemistry in our bodies, rather than by some vaguely esoteric exterior influences. Oh, yes, there is "psychology," there is a major potential from the mind. But do not discount the descending genes and chromosomes and all such as that. If you have had the right kind of parents, you are almost certain to triumph over any adversity that environment can toss at you. Never mind the tragedy of the preacher's children who "go astray"; many preachers are bums behind their unctuous façades.

Thus it was inevitable that the five surviving children of Will and Archie Arnold turned out reasonably well. I shall now etch brief portraits of the first four. You can make your own deductions about the fifth.

I wish you could have seen us in those 1900-to-1920 years!

Seven Irish folk—no, eight, because Uncle Johnny Barry was there —in one big white house on a hill, *living*! Living, mind you, not just existing. Some allegedly wise analyst has said that the majority of human beings live lives of quiet desperation. I doubt that, but if it is true, we were in the minority. Oh, we had our problems, our troubles, our financial and physical and emotional stringencies, but we also were endowed with at least one matchless weapon for fighting back. That was a sort of defiant self-reliance. Individually and collectively, we challenged any bugaboos that dared bare their fangs at us; we did not trot whining to the government. Yes, occasionally those bared fangs got us—we were not immortal—in which case we licked our wounds and limped onward until we were healed again. We could do that because of the mental toughness that I have already mentioned, a toughness tempered always with tenderness.

Oldest brother William Tip Arnold was like that.

TIP

I first saw Tip—or rather, Tip first saw me, according to our mother—before we had left that log home down in the village of Minden. Tip had been "out West" for months hoping to regain his health. No, not from tuberculosis, but some strange intestinal thing. As a young man he had come home to visit and there was his baby brother at age two upended in the kitchen flour barrel.

Never mind how I got there. I have no idea. No doubt I just climbed up unseen and somehow toppled. But they said that Tip lifted out a tiny squawling white ghost and started laughing.

Tip is still laughing when he comes into focus for my first memory picture of him, because he had been cracking a joke in the back porch family gathering in Henderson. Laughter is a part of Irish life. A deeper truth is, laughter is a main concomitant of successful living by anybody, anywhere, any time.

We The People of America, nursing a heritage from the grim Puritans, did not appreciate the value of wholesome humor for our first 300 or so years. Today, virtually all topflight psychologists, psychiatrists, sociologists, clergymen, and other authorities tell us that a clean sense of humor is equal in value to a sense of morals. They remind us that God himself obviously has a sense of humor, because He made us in his image, didn't he, and man has one? There are 252 examples of humor in the Holy Bible. Irrevocably, humor is the calisthenics of the mind.

TIP

Big brother Tip Arnold would never have phrased that philosophical concept in any such manner. Nevertheless it was plain that he subscribed to it as did all of our Irish family, including our Negro friends. Tip probably was the best yarn spinner and joke teller in Henderson. And his funnyisms never, never held a sting.

When he went back to West Texas he caught a little cage full of striped ground squirrels and shipped them to me by railway express. He didn't have to do that; he simply loved a baby brother with whom he had enjoyed very little association. I kept those pets for years.

A few months after they arrived, Mr. Bob Gould, the station agent at the I. & G. N. (International and Great Northern) depot, telephoned me.

"Oren," he boomed it, as he always did in talking, "you better get down here, boy. You have a pony here, a Shetland pony. Tip sent it to you from out near Abilene. It's in the express car in a crate. Get on down here and ride it home. It's in our way."

"WHOO! Yes, *sir!*"

I yelped the news to Mama and Sis and the others, then took off at Olympic speed; or, as Mama phrased it, lickety-split.

Sure enough, there was my pony. A diminutive roan with glassy yellow eyes, a long mane, and longer swishy tail. Even a bridle.

We got him out of the crate and down a ramp onto the cinder-strewn area there, where old ranch-reared me, a genu-wine cowboy already, magnificently grabbed "holt" of the bridle reins over his neck and swung up, bareback.

ka-POW!

Some fifteen or twenty Negroes and white people, including my family, who had gathered to see the new pony, now watched me sail upward six feet or so and land skidding in those locomotive cinders.

All right. Tip of the generous heart had loved me enough to buy me a Shetland and ship him to me. So after I got over the abrasions on my skin and my psyche, I led that husky critter out onto a soft, freshly-plowed field and "broke" him. I mean, I got on and got put off until we both tired of it, and finally he just trotted around and let me stay on his back. My brother Grady did the coaching; made me get back on each time I was dumped. "There never was a rider that couldn't be throwed," quoth Grady, reversing the ancient ranch axi-om, "and there never was a horse that couldn't be rode."

The roan Shetland enriched my next eight years. I rode him often to school and, because of him, was the center of attention there. Girls fawned over me and boys hated me, and I enjoyed it all.

Tip, then, shared his goodness. Not only with me and the rest of his homefolks, but with outsiders as well. Pretty soon he was courting a town beauty named Norma Arnold, daughter of that attorney, John R. Arnold, no kin of ours. And what he himself thought of as "hu-mor" entered into that courtship. For instance, he caught a three-foot-long coachwhip, put it in a shoebox and paid a Negro boy a dime to deliver it to Miss Norma.

Now a coachwhip will grow up to eight feet or so long and still be no larger than your finger. It is utterly harmless to man, lives on field mice and insects and such like. But in hunting, it will raise its head up maybe two feet and look around and thereby scare the absolute Yid-dish bejabbers out of anybody who happens to see him and is afraid of snakes anyway. That includes me. So I do not blame Miss Norma for exploding. She wouldn't let Tip Arnold even enter her front yard for a month, even if everybody else in town did think the matter was hilarious.

He finally sent her a fine puppy and a big armload of roses and a two-dollar box of candy (five pounds, brought in all the way from Dallas) and followed that up with a lot of sweet talk over our hall telephone, which all the people on our party line gleefully enjoyed. His wheedling got through to her, and she let him come calling again.

When they got married, in a whopping grand "society" wedding, he gave her a choice: she could have a fine diamond ring, or she could have a fine rubber-tired buggy pulled by a gorgeous high-stepping stallion named Ernest. Norma was no fool, she chose Ernest and the rig, and all of Henderson nodded approval. Tip and Norma were off to a heavenly start.

Their life story, regrettably, became a sad one. That ancient bugaboo, ill health, assailed them, and prosperity could not lick it. Much too soon, Norma passed on, and Tip was inconsolable. Many years passed before he finally married again.

But back there in his younger years he and Norma had built them a fine home about two hundred yards from our big white one, and *it* was open to all comers all the time. A baby was born, Virginia. The same Virginia who, in the 1960's, helped establish that library in her John Arnold grandfather's honor; the same Virginia to whom this book is dedicated, and whose home in Rusk County is still as "open" to all comers as those before her were, and whose heart carries on the family traditions.

Equally vivid in my memory is Tip's handling of what he came in later years to call his Colored Colony. By shrewd buying and building, he became owner of sixty small dwellings in what today would be tagged an Oppressed Area and would stir up futile ecological recriminations. Actually it was built in a pretty woodland along a tinkling, twinkling, silvery brook created by a natural spring. He got ten to fifteen dollars a month rental for those sixty houses, which totaled a grand monthly income. But his manner of living was almost starkly plain, because he channeled most of his money back into charities. Mistuh Tip Arnold—he Mistuh Will's son—was a sort of walking godfather to the residents in the Colored Colony.

No, he did not fraternize with them unduly. No, he did not allow himself to become fatuously condescending. He simply stayed his own honest self, going there as need be to collect the rents or to hire workers or whatever, petting a few babies, teasing a few bigger children, swapping a few jokes with the men, then going on about his white man's business. So a mutual respect held. Almost every week one of the colored friends would bring him produce from gardens, or maybe a brace of wild squirrels shot from trees, or a huge catfish caught on a trotline, or a gallon of those wild plums I mentioned. All in all, Tip died a happy man eventually, rising above sadnesses and troubles caused by ill health. He held no grudge against life.

And that last statement is probably the finest epitaph I could write for him.

BUCK

Buck Arnold was the next child, but he was a horse of another color. He had subtleties of refinement that Tip lacked, due unquestionably to his better health. For one thing, he was larger boned, taller, blessed—or burdened, being a boy—with luscious curly hair that made the maidens drool. Obviously, Mama beheld beauty in him that very first week of his life, because she named him Jewel—of all things! Thomas Jewel. Under other circumstances he might well have grown up as another sweet little Lord Fauntleroy. But Mama had more sense than to allow that so, when the boy was a two-year-old and acting real "bucky," she made no protest when Papa nicknamed him Buck. After all, a he-man type is better than a pretty sissypants. The nickname stuck; nobody ever referred to him as Thomas or Jewel, although in time little nieces called him Jubuck. And, years later, by sheer coincidence he married a beauty whose real name was Miss Buck; first name, Georgia.

His exploits as a farm lad and as a highly capable teenager are legendary in our family but too many for presenting here. He seems to have been the most "solid" one of us children. He looked distinguished, it was said, even before he was sixteen and, by the time he was a practicing attorney, he both looked and acted like a statesman. He whizzed through high school as if it were a petty nuisance with barely enough stimulus to interest him, then went on to Austin, found

BUCK

a room in historic B Hall at The University of Texas there, got a job waiting on tables in the dining room, and put himself through law school.

Great! Small wonder we were all proud of Buck. A self-made attorney, who lived to be past eighty, and who even at that point of decrepitude could wallop my tail every time him and me played golf at the Houston Country Club, of which he was president. And I am not a bad golfer, myself. Twice, Buck even got a hole-in-one, the louse; and lorded it over me.

Back there in those pre-1920 years Buck was already a sort of family hero and leader. Generous to a fault, he big-brothered me so that I was (by my sister allegedly) "spoiled," a condition I thoroughly enjoyed. He slipped me as many dimes as Uncle Johnny Barry did. Better yet, Buck habitually talked with me. I mean, he both talked and listened; he was more like a father than Papa was, because he was psychologically more modern, more understanding.

Wasn't that listening a wonderful form of heart outreach?

I submit that it was; that it was as wonderful as our parents' constant welcome for friends, kin, and strangers. You who today have little brothers or sisters, or children of your own, take heed. Talk to them often, yes, but more important—listen to them, so that they can air their problems and confusions and you can help them set a true course. Buck did that instinctively, first with younger brothers Grady and me, then with his own tribe of kids and grandkids. I never saw him angry, or indignant, or disturbed. He couldn't have been "preachy" if he had tried. He simply had a matchless heart understanding. Even when I talked to him about pretty Mary-Margaret Sara O'Reilly who, momentarily, was my all-and-everything.

However, he also was something of a happy-go-lucky Irish rascal. Let me relate what he done—did—one night before our teen-age sister Opal was married. Sis always had a crowd of youths around her; a magnificent smile, flanked by two deep dimples, plus a laughing, outgoing personality in every other way, guaranteed that. On this occasion four town girls were spending the night with her by bedding down on pallets in her room. Nobody used her bed; the floor was more fun for one night.

You can imagine most of it, I am sure. The fudge-making. The incessant chatter. The eternal giggling and cutting up. All that. But midnight did come, and fatigue did set in, and they did eventually all go to sleep there on the floor, so the house became quiet. To escape their clatter I had already left my room and gone to a cot on the back porch, feeling contemptuous.

But come two A.M. or so—*scra-a-aa-ape*, BANG!

A horrendous noise awoke all of us. Something had made it just outside the north window of sister's room. I heard the girls screech in terror. I sat up on my cot, also alarmed.

No more sound came. An animal? Maybe a crazy owl, flying into the window screen? One guess was as good as another. The house quieted down again, but ten minutes later the harsh sound was repeated. Mama got up and lit a lamp, and Buck, upstairs, got out of his bed in his long nightgown and came to the head of the stairs and asked Mama what was the matter and should he come down and investigate. Mama said no, it probably was just some town boys teasing the girls, but Buck solemnly told her and the girls that there had been a crazy man loose around Henderson lately, and there was no tellin' what he might do. Even so, Mama ordered all of us back to our beds.

Nobody slept much. But I got up early and snuck around outside Sis's room to see what I might find.

I found that brother Buck, whose room was just over hers, had tied six neckties into a rope and attached an old shoe to the end of it. He had been banging that against her window. The rascal.

One September there, Baylor University sent a picturebook creature to Henderson to be a teacher in our high school. Big brother Buck discovered her, and right away lightning struck.

I mean, he came home looking loopy and glassy eyed, dazed and disoriented. His sudden infatuation with her did nothing to endear the new Miss Georgia Buck to the Henderson girls, but who cared about that? Love is love, and nothing else matters.

I can see it all now. Dang it all, I was critically hacked because be dogged if I didn't draw this Miss Buck as teacher in my history and German classes. I was ready to leave town; maybe go join the Navy after all. For I would surely get the backwash of town talk about Buck and Georgia.

Then I sort of come to my senses. If I was her fiance's little brother, I could expect to have some favors in history and German class. Wasn't that reasonable?

No go. I tell you, that pretty teacher leaned backward being strict with me; I couldn't get by with nothing! One day she even made me and Tunk Griffin stay in after school for two whole hours just to memorize a stinkin' German poem. But I learnt it! I can recite it even now, more than half a century later:

> *Du bist wie eine Blume*
> *So hold und schön und rein—*

and so on for six more lines.

Here in the 1960's and 1970's I have frequently used that opening line. In Germany itself. Whenever I encounter a pretty young waitress there, I say it to her, first thing. Invariably she blushes, giggles, and gives me and Adele impeccably prompt and perfect service. So children, it pays to learn your lessons in school!

Him and her up and got married and they settled in Houston (Don't be upset by my use of the vernacular now and then, friends. You wouldn't want me to make this book a dull, scholarly thing like a doctoral thesis or a report in The Congressional Record.) Pretty soon I growed up enough to need some college learnin', so big-hearted Buck talked me into trying out for Rice Institute, now Rice University, one of the toughest schools in the world to get into. Somehow or other, I made it. Papa sent me there with two hundred dollars, Buck slipped me ten bucks now and then, and I got a job making fifteen a week as campus reporter for the *Houston Chronicle*; so I became a plutocrat. But I also became baby-sitter for Buck and Miss Georgia, inasmuch as The Pill had not yet been invented.

I enjoyed all of that. Mainly because I discovered that Miss Georgia had really loved me all the while. No longer my teacher, but my big sister, she made up for lost time. One day Dr. Stockton Axson, the great Shakespearean scholar, told us in his class at Rice that Shakespeare had said, "They do not love, who do not *show* their love." I thought hard on that, and realized that my Papa and Mama had been showing it—not merely mouthing it—for years, and that now my new sister-in-law was showing it to me.

She and Buck aged along and had five children, and I am happy to report that they caught the gleam. Here in the 1970's, Billy Buck and Mary Virginia and Tom and Dan and dainty Jane, the baby, all are married and happy in the programming of their own heart outreach. All have big fine homes that are as "open" as was that of their paternal grandsire who threw away his front door key. Isn't life wonderful, sometimes? I mean, as when the good aspects of it are handed down from generation to generation?

Those Buck Arnold children were never "lectured" about doing Good Works, any more than the Will Arnold children had been. All concerned, in both generations, simply grew up in an environment and routine where selflessness seemed automatic. Nobody was surprised, or even made any comment on it, when Buck Arnold, in Houston, prospered as an oil attorney, then expanded his altruism by reaching Back Home. One by one he brought a family of extremely poor Negro children from a family in Rusk County all the long way down to Houston. In turn, he gave them a home in a clean and comfortable apartment over his double garage. One by one, he put them through high school and college. And one by one he saw each of them become outstanding citizens of the South, men and women who are making reputations for themselves, not as militants *demanding* equality with white Americans by threatening or using violence, but as Christians, happily leading their own lives, and working with all groups for a common ideal.

Buck did not tell anyone about that. Not for years did we Arnolds upstate even suspect it. When we did hear, no big thing was made of his philanthropy. It was simply that Buck had prospered, had made a fortune, so *of course* he would share it. What was more natural than for him to reach back to his homeland and help lift the level of needy ones there? He did not merely write checks, he took direct personal interest. Such was his heritage.

OPAL

Never overburdened with modesty anyway, I have repeatedly bragged about my big Sis. So I blithely repeat now that my sister Opal was the second most beautiful teenage girl I ever saw. (I married a teenager, and I am no fool!) Physically, she had inherited everything a girl child needed.

By being the only girl in the family, she undoubtedly gathered too much attention and got too many favors. I recall that whenever Tip, Buck, Grady, or I wanted something special, or costly, from Papa, we did not ask him direct; we diplomatically conned Sis into asking for us. Invariably, the results were good. Even Ellen the cook favored Miss Opal. But Mama saw to it that the girlish personality was kept reasonably well balanced, and that enabled Sis to acquire the parental penchant for kindness and selfless love.

A somewhat doddery old kid in her eighties now, and still flashing those two deep, deep dimples with her smiles, she rules the roost for the family in Henderson. Partial deafness has afflicted her, as it has me. But that simply makes all the children and grandchildren and friends talk louder, thereby emphasizing many good things that she does. She bakes cakes for her pastor, and he comes by to shout his thanks, forgetting that she has a good hearing aid. She takes soup to the sick, she drives people to hospitals when needed—though she shouldn't, because she rolls right up the middle of any street; nothing happens, because all the town people know her car and in deft self-preservation, pull far to one side, then wave as she passes and shout

"Hi, Miss Opal!" She shells out money for charity; she will give any needy Negro matron a full layette for a new babe; she "belongs" to two churches but does not try to run either of them; she plays a cut-throat game of bridge, gambling as much as a whole quarter during an afternoon, and likely winning, and giving the winnings to some barefoot urchin she encounters on the way home. Each midmorning she loads her car with friends and drives a mile to the fine restaurant operated by our Cousin "Buddy" Dawson, goes back into his kitchen and visits with the cooks, tells Buddy how things should be done— while he dutifully and happily says "Ah shuah do appreciate your tell-ing me all this, ma'am." Buddy, the lovable hypocrite, has heard it every day for years, but always pretends. And whenever Sis and her companions sit at a table, they get instant impeccable service, from the proprietor himself. Usually all they want is cake, coffee, and conver-sation. They should omit the cake; each one of these fine old Hender-son women is a trifle paunchy now, but Buddy pretends not to see that. Invariably, there is a hassle about the check; Buddy never brings one, but Sis and her gang demand one, and finally just go away leav-ing money on the table. Life in Henderson hasn't really changed too much in these sixty-odd years.

As a fine, sweet, considerate, modest, loving and lovable little-boy brother of Opal away back there, I never could understand why she so often felt it necessary to chase me and hit at me, or something. Not that we ever *fought*; Mama would not hear to such deportment. But, you know. It always has been inherent, instinctive, inevitable, for lit-tle brothers to nag big sisters. I recall that our porch and parlor were eternally overrun with Town boys, so I felt duty bound to horn in. I was not welcome.

"Ma-ma, make Oren stay away, can't you?" Thus the eternal cry, which I suppose is an ageless, universal pattern in millions of homes.

Later, I saw her own devilish son, Billy Preston, now a distin-guished adult citizen and financier in Henderson, nag Opal's own lovely daughters, Ruth and Eugenia, when it was *their* turn to float around a big home with retinues of boys. Moreover, I have since seen her grandchildren repeat the formula, and seen it again in my own home with my three beautiful daughters and more lately with my four beautiful granddaughters.

Back there in the mauve decade, the soft years from 1900 to 1910, nobody traveled much. Hence, distance lent enchantment. We heard about, and read about and talked about, far places with glamorous names. Then one day, into our county-seat metropolis of eighteen hundred souls, came a character named Edward Massenburg Preston. Called Ned.

He had come to Henderson direct from Paris! Even when we learned that he meant Paris, Texas, his mystique did not fade, because it also developed that he, with his parents, had actually lived in New York City itself! Could anybody possibly ask for more than that?

Sis couldn't, so she married him.

At first, his courtship threatened to set up the stereotyped city-slicker-and-farmer's-daughter, in real life. Papa disapproved of handsome, suave, courteous young Ned, and said so. That Ned boy was not solid. He even run one of these newfangled roller-skating rinks in town, and there was no tellin' what all went on there. No, Sis could not marry him.

Mama seemed to hold the matter in abeyance. Wise Ellen Austin put heavy hands on fat hips, looked worried but ruled that "Miss Opal, she ain't likely to do nuthin' wrong," and wise old Uncle Johnny Barry murmured, "That's so." Sis paid no attention to any of them; no really self-respecting, high-spirited Irish girl would have, or should have.

She married up with him on December 20, 1910—at exactly eleven o'clock in the morning.

And, bless Jesus, at exactly eleven o'clock every morning for the remainder of his life, no matter where he was, he either telephoned or visited the woman he always called "Doll." If any morning at that hour the Board of Directors of his insurance or his savings and loan association business was in solemn session, Ned, the president, would quietly take a five-minute recess to telephone. The other men, smiling gently, approved and waited; sometimes one would say, "Give our love to Miss Opal."

Or, if winter was on, he might just drive the five blocks to their home at 11 o'clock and put fresh wood on their fireplace blaze, maybe a big new backlog, then chat with Doll a few minutes as they watched the crackling sparks. The rest of the family, including the servants,

learned just to let the morning fire die down so as not to deny him that privilege and pleasure. The big home was well heated with a furnace, but that fireplace had symbolic importance, as most fireplaces do. About eleven-twenty he would go back to the office, to return again for lunch at twelve and kiss her in greeting as if he hadn't seen her since last June. All that, mind you, continued even when both had become gray-haired senior citizens. Truly, love *is* a many-splendored thing.

On that December day in 1910 people said that the marryin' was beautiful, what with the incubator taken out of the parlor and lots of

flowers and stuff stacked in there. I wouldn't know, I never seen it; saw it. Immature skeeter that I was, I hid upstairs during the ceremony and cried. I don't know why; I thought Ned Preston hung the moon *and* the stars.

It turned out that he nigh about did, too. Theirs was among the happiest, most successful marriages and subsequent family lives that I have ever observed or heard of. Never mind any long discourse about it, it's just that each party to it was a spiritual gem. Ned must have had parents as wonderful as my own, for there was nothing—repeat, *nothing*—that he wouldn't do for you. You didn't even have to ask; in time of need, anybody's need, it seemed that he was always there, already helping do battle against any dragon. It got so the town people depended on him. They came to him for advice and guidance. They tried to run him for mayor; he refused, saying he lacked the qualifications, which was an erroneous statement. He prospered in insurance, then in a new savings and loan association, which he founded with several close friends. The association dominates the town's business structure to this day, with his widow, my elderly Sis, as its nominal head. She "goes to the office" every morning, even now, and makes what she regards as a close inspection of business procedures and decisions. This consists of finding the building janitor—an old and trusted friend, near her age—then sitting with him back in the little coffee kitchen and chatting about old times. They speak often of Ned Preston. Most likely, other old timers will drop in, sip the brew, and reminisce. It is a wonderful way to keep control of a thriving financial institution, and her son Billy, her son-in-law, M. J. Pipsaire, and her daughter Eugenia, the real officers in charge, encourage her in it. They all call her Sis. Many of the town people call her Sis, or Miss Sis, sometimes Miss Opal. If a man calls her Mrs. Preston, everyone knows he is a newcomer to town.

Have I, again, made my point, for you dear hearts and gentle readers? Is it clear that the grand tradition is still very much alive?

GRADY

You, being well read, versed in history and all that, of course know all about a once famous statesman-humanitarian in the Old South by the name of Henry W. Grady.

GRADY

Well, the brother next above me was named for him; by a mother who doubtless hoped that some of the great one's attributes might miraculously come to live in the heart of her child.

And, in some ways, they really did.

Daniel Grady Arnold might well have become a statesman. He did become a humanitarian, by making himself into a physician. Regrettably, my memory of his boyhood years with us is rather dim, possibly because those were my least impressionable years, and by the time I had acquired some perceptivity, he was up and gone to Austin, taking his premed courses. After that, he had a hard four years in The University of Texas Medical School at Galveston. But I got to visit him down there! As a knee-pants kid, I stayed right in his dorm room with him, and he introduced me around to all the doctors and nurses and professors, just as if I was his equal. For a whole week. That really set me up. It was more wonderful than plunging into the Gulf of Mexico surf, right across the street there. All of it was unforgettable evidence of Grady Arnold's kindness. It also revealed to me that he had a gift, a zest for living matched by few people in our world. I never knew him to show any hint of despair. Even when, years later, he, as a doctor, knew that he was dying, he faced his Hereafter with a quiet kind of eagerness and a gentle smile.

From bits that I picked up here and there, I know he must have been quite the fair-haired kid in college. His crinkly hair and devilish grin would surely have made the Longhorn coeds swoon, even if he hadn't been a "divine" dancer, which same he was. At the U he acquired the nickname "Chinky," because in his freshman year I mailed him a big box full of black sweet-meated "chinky-pins" and most of the students had never heard of them before, but were much taken with them. Also, I believe it was he who won the freshman honors in tennis that year, which helped him toward prominence. That same Mr. Bittle who "learnt" me the game had also learnt Buck and Grady. Papa wouldn't let Sis try to learn; any girl with lovely legs—pardon me, I mean limbs—should never flaunt them by leaping around in coltish fashion. But Buck and Grady became tennis experts.

Grady made high grades as a novice medico, I recall. Ellen, our surrogate mother, told the world that "Mistuh Grady, he already de bes' doctuh in Texas." Shucks, he hadn't even got his diploma yet, but we all rather agreed with her. We swelled even more when he went to the big hospital in the East to expand his knowledge.

Back there, a hellish epidemic of Spanish influenza laid him low. Weakened severely, he finally came on home to "rest up and recuperate."

In barely thirty days, Dr. Daniel Grady Arnold was the favored son of the town. His first patient was Mama herself. He knew she had been suffering continual pain for almost a year, so he asked me privately what had been done for her.

"Well, Dr. White come," I recalled. "Three times, I guess."

"What did he do for her?"

"He sat in a rocking chair and asked Mama to stick out her tongue. She was in *her* rocker across the room. But she stuck it out, and he peered at it over his glasses, and left some calomel for her to take all three times. They visited some too."

"Good lord! Go tell her to come in here, right now." We were already in her room. When she arrived he ran me out and told me to guard the door for half an hour.

When they reappeared he told us that he was taking her to the hospital in Galveston tomorrow. He did just that, although it distressed all of us. Down there they removed a growth—something vague, to me; possibly a malignancy—which the doctors said saved her life. Right away the whole town heard about it and Grady's reputation soared.

Whereupon the four old doctors in the town gleefully retired and went fishin'. They had yearned to do that anyway. Now here was Will Arnold's boy doctoring, so let him do the work. One other good new doc had come to town, Dr. Shaw. Together they could handle things, it was hoped. Both were soon swamped. For some months, my brother averaged next to no sleep at all, each twenty-four hours. Mama would put him to bed whenever possible, day or night. But in half an hour, sure as shootin', the dang telephone would ring, and conscience forced her to awaken him.

"Abby Carter is about to deliver," she told him one morning, typically. "Hurry." They had already known that Abby's time was near.

Abby lived eleven miles from town on an unpaved road. Grady phoned Alicia, a lively, wealthy, and sophisticated town girl, to meet him on her curb, picked her up, and roared out to the Carter farm. Such dashing rides as this were about the only times he could find to court Alicia and, believe me, she was worth courting. She was merely the prettiest girl that I had ever—*wait a minute!* I do get carried away, remembering feminine beauties, but I'll just stick to Adele as first, my Sis second, with Alicia a close third. She was to wait in the car at the Carter farm while Grady worked his clinical magic, as per their established routine. So pretty soon he went into the farm house and left her reading a magazine.

Sure enough, the prospective mother was moaning in agony, he reported to us later. In and near her bedroom stood her husband, her mother, mother-in-law, and assorted other family members, all long-faced with worry. Grady quickly shucked his coat, rolled his shirt sleeves, sterilized his hands as best he could, said a few comforting words to the lady in labor, then pulled her bed covers down and her gown up so that he could appraise the situation.

At that instant he felt a hard punch in his back.

Startled, he turned. There stood Abby's husband with his finger on the trigger of a shotgun. "It ain't no man gonna look at my wife naked," he snarled. "Not even no doctor."

Since then, I have heard of comparable instances. It seems that the sanctity of womanhood—call it that—had prompted such feelings in many a husband across rustic America. I have even learned of an almost identical instance in North Dakota. And I think that paternal reaction has sort of become legendary.

But it was very real there for Grady. For a long moment everybody seemed to freeze. After all, a gun is a gun, and murder was a finger squeeze away. What to do?

Grady had no time for what might be called rational thinking, we all agreed later. He simply reacted from instinct. He looked that belligerent farmer in the eye and spoke to him.

"Mr. Carter, I was called here by you, to deliver your child and if possible to save its life and that of your wife. I have taken an oath to do the best I can in any emergency, and believe me this is one. Her pelvis is too small, she may die in childbirth. Now instead of shooting me, I suggest that you pray for God to guide my hands. If you are too mean to do that, then go ahead and shoot." Whereupon the doctor went back to his duty, ignoring the spectators behind him.

Well, once Papa had taken a pistol from a man who had sworn to kill him. Now Papa's son also faced a killer's gun. And each had reacted with singular courage.

No shot was fired. A few minutes later Mr. Carter had put down his shotgun and was quietly sobbing, then he went on out to his barn. The women folk began heating water unnecessarily and getting in each other's way and saying that there is a mighty fine young doctor.

But matters were worse than Grady had suspected. Grady rushed to the front door. "ALICIA!" he yelped. "Come in here quick!"

Surprised, the dainty and sweet and prettily attired girl ran to him with a questioning look.

"I need help desperately. Don't you dare act skittish, don't faint or do anything silly like that. Come on in here and do exactly as I say."

About an hour later, very untrained nurse Alicia, looking pale but firm-lipped, quietly started with Dr. Arnold back to their car. Doc called back to the Carter people. "Yes, a fine healthy baby, and Abby will be in good shape by Sunday. I'll drop back tomorrow. Goodbye for now. Get in, Alicia."

She had not fainted or faltered. She had come of strong stock, even as the doctor had. They did not speak much of their adventure, but merely reported it as somewhat more than routine. Incidentally, nobody ever paid either of them for that call; the Carters had too little money to live on, much less "wasting" any of it on a doctor or a nurse.

Much of his service in Rusk County did become charity work. Even so, he made money, more than a single man needed for those years. I recall some talk about taxes back there, between Sheriff Joel Hale, Uncle Johnny, brother Buck the lawyer, Papa, and Dr. Grady. The talk was casual, but sincere.

"They have saddled us with what they call a federal income tax," Sheriff Hale lamented. "It will take some of your money, Grady."

"Yes, sir, I guess so."

"Well, let it," my wise Papa ruled. "They have promised us that the tax will never be more than two percent. Surely we owe that much to our government." Papa, you will remember, had been a tax assessor for the county, himself. He knew whereof he spoke.

"That's so," avowed Uncle Johnny, and the rest of us nodded sagely. The federal income tax would never be over two percent; the government had promised! Dear God! Dear, dear God.

Grady never married Alicia. Before the year was out he "broke down" with tuberculosis, brought on by overwork and lack of rest. He went out to El Paso and entered Homan Sanatorium, lying flat on his back for weeks. But the next thing we knew, he was up and practicing in the sanatorium as head of its extensive TB ward, and when I visited him out there—myself a grown-up young man by then —he was engaged to a lovely fellow patient named Helen, who had lived in Galveston.

They never got married, either. That TB is a treacherous thing, any time. Grady did decide he was cured one day, so he returned to East Texas and set up an x-ray laboratory in Tyler. It was interesting to see our country people's reaction to that. Quite a few million Americans just then did not "believe in" x-rays. Asafetida bags, yes, because these had been handed down from grandmama's time as sure preventions of diseases. (Those repulsive little necklace bags really worked, too. Their odor was so incredibly horrid that everybody, including people with infectious ailments, stayed far away from you!) But those newfangled x-ray things were too mysterious, said the earnest country folk; yet if Will Arnold's boy was using them——. The net result was confusion.

Grady had come along as one of the New Era scientists. Prior to 1900, the authorities tell us here in the 1970's, the sum total of human knowledge had been doubling roughly every hundred years, but by 1970 it was doubling every five years. You will recall that our guest boy, Jon Demosthenes Blaine, spoke knowledgeably of that acceleration, which had already begun. Thus he and Grady both sensed and encouraged the newness in the world.

Grady was definitely innovative. Most people even today tend to resist newness, worshiping the status quo; they prefer to ride the train of tested thought and do what has been done. Back there in Grady's time that attitude was even more prevalent, so that his x-ray—and many other new techniques in doctoring—gave him a prominence. Unquestionably, he was a scientist whose mind was hospitable to new ideas, which always is the ultimate hospitality.

He died suddenly, of overwork again. We learned that he had channeled most of his money into avenues for helping destitute TB sufferers; also that brother Buck helped in this by sending him money of his own. Chinky and Buck. Texans, who rode tall in their saddles.

I am a better man for having been their little brother.

 # Animal People

As I pause here, restudying what I have written, harking back and meditating, I realize that people have been marching before you in a sort of continuing Texas parade. And such people! Without fame or fortune, without bombs or bombast, they are more "storybook" than those in the fiction stories, if you get to know them.

Now I interrupt their parade to present some nonhuman characters who are just as real, because they, too, help me develop my main theme here—that love and generosity, the open-heart syndrome, is the only insurance for happiness on this earth. Nonhuman? That means, of course, our animal life, including wildings from forest and field. In the routine of our living during those first decades of this century, animals were far more important than they are in the mechanized artificiality of today.

I have already mentioned some of ours by name. Mama's great white gelding Tom, for instance. That horse seemed more benevolent than Papa himself. I think God must have made Tom half human; a kind of spiritual centaur. Twice at least, Tom backed his ears, extended his neck and head, then galloped to defend me, a careless twerp of a child, from animals that might have killed me. One was a boar whose tushes, protruding around his snout, were as long as my middle fingers; the other was a mean young mule that leaped toward me, pawing. Do you wonder that we loved Tom?

Six little kids could ride him at once. Six! The front one had to straddle his neck; the last one clung to the fifth one so as not to slide down that snowbank of rump and tail. Then, when we were all ready, we all did slide down that snowbank and Tom appeared to enjoy it as much as we. He could run like a racer if ever he or Mama wanted him to. But with children on his hurricane deck, he slow-motioned a sedate clop–clop–clop, lifting his knees high and keeping his neck arched as if he were in a circus. Surely he understood; surely he loved us as much as we loved him. Frequently lumps of dark, grainy sugar-cane candy did nothing to alienate his affections, of course; he would even come up the kitchen steps to beg those from Ellen.

As me and Bonny Flanagan grew big—like, say, age ten or eleven —we could imitate those marvelous riders in Gentry Brothers Dog and Pony Show that came to our town each year, erecting its tent in Cover's Pasture. Our mamas made us handsome "tights." Mine were simply outgrown long winter underwear dyed red, but somebody had sewed fancy spangles on Bonny's, which was right and proper. We learned to stand up on Tom while he circused around a circle in our broad side yard near the porch with the well. We would charge other kids a whole nickel to see that and allied circus acts, including Bonny's stunts on my trapeze, and a few tricks by my dog, Rags. Sometimes we had as many as ten in our grandstands—planks stretched across empty nail kegs or fireplace logs. I swear it—Tom horse enjoyed acting in a circus as much as me and Bonny did.

When he eventually died of old age, Mama and Sis and I all cried, and both Tip and Papa were solemn as we hitched a team of mules to his carcass and drug—dragged—it a mile back to the far peach orchard and buried him in a deep gully. Most dead animals we simply took away somewhere for the buzzards to enjoy, and later the bones could be absorbed as fertilizer in the soil. But not Tom. He was a member of our family.

No other horse was loved as much. Yet there were several, probably twenty or more altogether, that we valued and respected highly, which I suppose is a form of love too. I have repeatedly mentioned the Shetland, Gypsy, that Tip sent me. But that diminutive pixie was more of a toy than a horse. I could ride him the mile to school and "horse around" with him at juvenile birthday parties and friends' homes and such. But in our world, riding meant that you swung astride a strong, intelligent beast that could and would carry you in hard work all day long, through rain and blizzards, hot suns and scorching winds, doing without water until nightfall if need be, sweating copiously with you or ducking his head against sleet, asking only for a pat on the neck when you finally unsaddled him, plus a stable with an arm load of hay and a dozen ears of shucked corn. Such creatures were valiant. Papa would have meted severe punishment to anybody who mistreated one of our fine saddle horses. And using them was a far richer experience than is today's barreling around in helicopters, trucks, and automobiles.

Matter of fact, I sort of pity today's cowboys. In terms of efficiency, they are far superior to us of the year 1915. Just a short time ago I visited a vast cattle-raising enterprise in California. With the boss I stood there on a hilltop and looked at 35,000 cattle in one herd. Imagine that—35,000 head of prime stock! Our ranch never had more than 500 or 600. The several cowboys in California each had a college degree in animal husbandry, each dressed, looked, and acted like the young scientist he was—a sharp contrast to the old whanghide cowpoke of our day in Texas. My host put about a hundred of those modern steers through a fancy chute and a cowboy scanned each ear-tag number, then reported it to a computer at his elbow. The beast was weighed automatically, and a card came out to show us his precise diet for the past month. If he hadn't gained enough, he was shunted left and would get a new ration. The expert cowboys there did have horses, but more often they sashayed around that vast ranch in helicopters. My Uncle Johnny, my brothers and that gifted Jon Demosthenes Blaine, my Papa, and George Austin, our foremen, would be astounded if they could see the overall modern mechanization. Modern ranching is a far cry from that in the days of the Chisholm Trail, or from that of the Will Arnold Big A brand. Incidentally, Papa's Big A branding iron hangs on my home porch today.

The city dweller today cannot possibly understand the closeness, the melding of personalities, that developed between a human being and his horse in long association. Since man first learned to domesticate the big animals, horsemen have been a superior clan. That was true in the pioneering of America, when the achievers rode westward and the ribbon clerks stayed secure in their womb-like homes. We are losing something as the horse gives way to autos and flying machines. You can not pet a Jeep.

George Austin was a genius with horses. He knew that to "break" a colt to the saddle you should never wait until it was grown, then get on and let it buck itself into frustration and exhaustion and mistrust of human beings. That always was the stupid way to do it. George would show us kids how to put a little blanket right on the week-old foal and get him used to that first. By degrees, we would add some weight to it, put on a little bridle, pet and fondle the creature, and get him completely accustomed to having human friends. Even mama mare always seemed to approve of such a technique, for she would rumble a few horse words of tenderness and nuzzle us, as well as her baby.

We had to let the little fellow go suck at least once an hour. A danged old calf, now, can suck a belly full of cow juice at dawn and get by with that until sundown, if need be. A colt, though, is a creature of much higher refinement, and his mama has no massive storage udder such as the cow has. Therefore, he grabs a teacupful when and as he can, from teats that are relatively short and fat, compared to mama cow's long ones.

Similarly, we soon hitched any baby colt to a little wagon. Maybe his eyes bulged in astonishment, even fear, at the harness strapped onto him. So we learned to sweet-talk him with sundry cooings and pettings, just as if he were a human babe. Pretty soon we'd have him walking proudly along pulling Bonny Flanagan's dolls in my play wagon and, in another few weeks, graduate him to a small two-wheeled cart on which a child could ride and hold the reins. From that, it was nothing to move the growing-up young animal into the shafts of a buggy, thence on into double harness beside a surrey tongue.

The keynote for all that? The modus operandi prescribed and enforced by Mama and Papa and George Austin?

Tenderness! That indispensable emotion, that same sweet outreach used on human beings.

Can you possibly smirk now, cynically saying that such a technique would never have been efficient on a real working ranch in the Wild West? If so, brother, you have been watching too many phony TV dramas, your brain is much too circumscribed.

By 1910 or so, it got to be quite a serious "joke" around Henderson that Will or Archie Arnold would skin you alive if you dared do any hunting on their domain. A few brash gun toters learned that the hard way, hence the word got spread.

That was our family attitude, even though we approved of hunting and fishing elsewhere and did a considerable amount of it. Papa instinctively developed our farm into a wildlife sanctuary. Once in a great while he would allow us to shoot a mess of blackbirds there near the barn, because they came in such profusion as to destroy tender crops. Anyhow, blackbird dumplin's can be even tastier than chicken dumplin's! Old King Cole himself knew about that. Our blackbirds were mostly pure satiny, shiny black, with only a chatter-raspy song. I could now wish they had been the red-winged species, for I have since

seen them swarm by the thousands in my yard at Phoenix, and their clear bell-like song at twilight creates a symphony richer than that of meadowlarks.

On the other hand, Papa inconsistently threw out buckets full of "chops"—cracked corn—just for the winged friends to eat, including swarms of those same greedy blackbirds. Don't ask me why. Is there any law that says human emotions have to be consistent?

Many a time I have seen that parent of mine swing a heavy sledge hammer onto a steer's forehead, busting the bone and slaying the animal right there in its tracks so that we could butcher it out for food and doing it while absent-mindedly whistling a little tune. Then I remember seeing him plowing a field one day, following two big mules with reins looped around his neck. Up front a few yards a mother bobwhite quail fluttered away. "Whoa," ordered Papa, and the mules gratefully stopped, blowing.

Papa walked the twenty yards ahead, looked down at a nest full of eggs, went to the fence row, cut four "stobs"—stakes about arm's length—and marked off a plot some twenty yards square for that mama bird to hatch and bring out her babies. He passed the word to all farm workers not to disturb that area, and nobody dared disobey.

On any farm or ranch, you *have* to kill. It is a law of survival, a part of God's plan, for us predators to prey on lesser beings. This is a reality the sentimental lovers-of-all-animals do not understand; yet I notice that almost none of them is a vegetarian.

George Austin protested several times when our barn feed lot got overrun with birds, I recall. The mental screen is in sharp focus there; even the audio is clear. A passel of chattering birds (I am not sure just how many units comprised what we called a passel) of all kinds had moved in on us. Any evenin'—afternoon—when me and maybe Grady or Otho or Draper or DeWitt or Jon came home from school and went out to start preparing feed for the working stock, we would find a reception committee lining the top fence rails and the side-boards of the troughs. If we were late, they would be fussing in pro-test—have you ever heard the fury of people today when occasionally their Social Security checks are late? Definitely, those birds were wait-ing for us, like lines of affluent loafers who have parked their Cadillacs and are queued before welfare offices today.

"You birds git on outa here," big George Austin would rumble, making shooing motions.

But he wouldn't mean it, and they well knew that. It was almost as if they grinned at him. Maybe a dozen bobwhites and two or three doves would offer token obedience, being shy types anyway. These would flap upward a few feet, pretending to be scared of George and us boys. Then they'd slip right back down, cock their heads at us—and wait. They could well have winged a hundred yards or so into the pastures or the fields which held abundant food for them. But they had come to prefer the more abundant life, even though it threatened to become "moribundant" for us. We even had a rich stand of milo maize down there near the pond, just right for birds. But no. Not at all. No more than many modern freeloaders accustomed to welfare will make more than a token effort to find a job. The birds had us well in hand. Sometimes they would even eat out of our hands, if we held the cracked corn out to them, pecking it with a lot of lovely sweet-talk thank-you cooings and fluttering and dancing around. Birds are smart, I tell you.

I had built us a big martin house, room for a dozen tenants, and set it high on a pole near Mama's chicken yard. No, not that I was such a bird lover, hooked on that particular species. That was in fact a nefarious counterattack on another species of feathered "friends"— I use the term loosely—the hawks.

It is something of a spectacle to witness a hawk appear out of the sky over your chicken yard when you have maybe five hundred adolescent and near featherless White Plymouth Rock chicks, their egg down just off, their few feathers not yet covering their bodies. Any danged hawk knows that one of them makes a super-delicious meal for himself and his own nestlings off somewhere among the trees. So down he comes, a dive bomber as deadly as any that Hitler flew.

The hens and roosters know about him, and do they ever let out a squawk! It amounts to a panic-alarm system, a blast of sirens. Even the little chicks are born knowing it by ear; hence, every fowl is terrified and dashes for cover. Most find it; or make it. I have seen little chicks and grown ones actually burrow under tufts of grass or into leaves if need be.

That's why we courted martins. Over the twenty years there I built at least six martin houses, and had pleasure doing it. I still see such houses in rural areas. Martins hate hawks as much as hens do, and *they* can counterattack and send the slower hawk fleeing ignominiously.

Papa, the strict conservationist at home, dearly loved to eat other people's wild birds, also their 'possums, rabbits, squirrels, fish, deer. I have never said that my Papa was perfect; not quite.

So then, life went on. Meanwhile, Mama, at her kitchen door, abetted by Ellen, took in any dog, cat, or wild beast too crippled or hungry to sustain itself. You talk about maintaining an "open house" —whoo! I have seen our big kitchen, warmed by the great wood-burning range, look more like an animal shelter than a place for human beings.

For years good dog Rags was the kingpin there. In the hierarchy of dogdom, he was far above other canine critters. Oh, he had no silly "pedigree." Yet he was as much an aristrocrat as was Will Arnold. There are pronounced strata in the society of most animals, no matter what human aficionados do with them, and old mixed-breed Rags stayed in the one on top. He literally ruled the place. Until one day that proud pooch, who had just knocked off a couple of yaller hounds in a fight, sniffed into a den of kittens. The little skinny mammy cat jumped on him, latched onto his neck and rode him while he raced a quarter mile, yelping. So take heed, people—pride goeth before a fall.

Rags seemed to like kittens. Once he found a stray one and brought it to Mama's kitchen, scratched the screen until she came and took the baby in. The kitten grew into a tomcat, and these two unlikely friends enjoyed close rapport for years.

Rags also was priceless with Mama's chickens. He was expert at sniffing out nests that dumb old hens tried to hide. If he missed one and the eggs hatched, he would guard it. If a rainstorm approached at night, he would sense the baby chicks' danger and come whining at our kitchen door, then lead somebody to them.

Rags licked anything or any person he loved. As instinct taught him to do, he also licked any injury to his body—and it got well. We close-to-nature folk all knew about the magic dog saliva. When any of us had, say, a runny boil or sore on a boyish leg, foot, arm, or wherever, just let Rags lick it several times. Invariably it promptly healed. Never mind about any feeling of cosmetic delicacy, and don't ask me, scornfully, how such a cure was possible. I do not know. I simply know that dog saliva has curative powers. Moreover, my knowledge is not mere folk superstition. Several years ago the eminent *Reader's Digest*—the most powerful periodical in man's history—carried an article reporting the truth about dog lick. But even it could not explain scientific details of the phenomenon.

In summation here—it is one thing to have a dainty French poodle lapkin in a chromium-coated condominium high above the streets of Dallas, Houston, or San Antone. But it is quite another to own a good tramp dog like Rags. Possibly I wouldn't mind being rich enough to own a pink poodle on which I'd have to spend a hundred bucks or so a month.

But if I did have that much money, I'd buy me a ranch and get me a Rags. As in the case of fine white horse Tom, such dogs do not ask to be pampered. Instinctively, they seem to know Nature's basic axiom—give love, in order to be loved.

 *Red-Letter Days*

At this point in our pageant of family living and loving you have met virtually all the dramatis personae. You have seen the parents, the children, the grandchildren, and assorted others in their real-life situations.

They constitute what modern members of the clan, harking back in moments of nostalgia, reliving the legends, refer to as "all those wonderful people." Truly they *were* wonderful. And the most wonderful aspect for me is that fate let me get in on the tag end of their drama—a boundless privilege. I know how memorable they were because I was there! And there are enough technicolored memories—of events and episodes, incidents and anecdotes, dialect and dialogue, actions and reactions—to fill ten books like this one. For instance, I have not even touched on the Festival Days in our farm and ranch living. I capitalize those words not because the Days were official, but because they were so grand. For most, I have room barely to mention, but two I must expand.

What we called "Juneteenth" stands out in memory, because we saw our Negro people make so much of it. On June 19, 1865, Union General Gordon Granger landed at Galveston and declared all Texas slaves free in accordance with the Emancipation Proclamation. In the vernacular of those given their freedom, Emancipation Day became "Juneteenth." Although somewhat biased Southerners, our family honored that Day. All our colored folk "took off" work. They could have any or every horse, buggy, wagon, and saddle we owned, for riding to picnics on that great holiday. Rigidly, Papa ordered all watermelons to be left alone in their fields, so that our Negro friends could have first picking on their Day. Once, when none was ripe enough, he slipped out in a wagon at night, bought twenty huge ripe ones from another farm, and next morning pretended to bring them in from our fields. That's Will Arnold for you; a white man on the black folks' day.

Generally we ignored July Fourth. We Texans had not been in the U.S.A. when the Declaration was signed. Moreover, it had been signed by a bunch of yankees anyway, so we just shrugged that one off. But we gave due deference to April 21, the anniversary of the day General Sam Houston won freedom from Mexico, setting up our proud Republic of Texas.

In my own time as a boy, there were political festival days. For instance, we would all "take off" when Jim Ferguson came to town. You have not heard of Jim Ferguson? I will not deign to detail his political career; just you ask any old-time Texan, the older the better, and be sure he is a Democrat. Papa would escort Jim around Town Square—and keep a sharp lookout ahead. Papa, spotting a particular citizen from our county, would hastily murmur facts to Jim. Big-hatted and hearty, Jim would approach the man with outstretched hand, saying, "Fate Welch! How are you, boy? How is Miss Addie, and those two fine children of yours? And are your truck gardens going well this year?" Lafayette Welch, called Fate, thus would be impelled to reelect Jim Ferguson as governor of Texas. Papa enjoyed that touch of hypocrisy in politics.

Christmas we took in stride, as I have already indicated. Easter, we dressed our best and went to church—and collected rabbit eggs that were laid mysteriously in our yard, until me and Bonny Flanagan aged up and became scornful. Then there was the annual Minden Picnic. On that occasion all of us Arnolds would try to go back to Maple Grove Church and cemetery near Minden, sing sacred harp music in the morning, eat huge amounts from dinner-on-the-ground, and help clean weeds and grass off the graves. A sweet and sad day for all.

But of all our festival days back there, I tend to think first and most of "surp makin' time."

We pronounced it that way—"surp." A few people, the literati of Texas, said "sur-up." Up North they spoke it more like "seer-up," which we considered an affectation. But then, what could you expect of yankees? If you were real down-to-earth and friendly and not try-ing to impress anybody with your erudition, you gave it the name that the Negroes used—'lasses. That's *mo*lasses in your dictionary. We left off the *mo*. A true story by that famous historian, John J. Apo-crapha, will illustrate:

"Please pass the 'lasses," one colored boy allegedly said at his family dinner table.

His uppity sister chided him, "You has to say *mo*-lasses."

He glared at her. "How come I has to say *mo*-lasses, when I ain't had none a-tall yit?"

What I am getting to—is that, come each autumn, with its colors glowing so marvelously in the sun-dappled woodlands of our "Bot-tom" farm, four miles south of the courthouse—a place apart from our acreage to the north—we all went down there on pilgrimages to the syrup mill.

Nine-tenths of you sophisticated moderns won't know what I am talking about. Syrup—molasses—has nothing to do with a "mill," has it? Syrup comes from, let me think, Hawaii isn't it? Or maybe Cuba, at least before Castro? What's a Texas syrup mill?

I don't really know what it is today when everything from sex to sin seems mechanized; don't even know if Texas has them anymore, although I am sure about some in neighboring Louisiana.

But a syrup mill is the apparatus used in making syrup out of cane.

Sugar cane grows in tall stalks, like bamboo. Papa and us "niggers" —we called ourselves that, black and white alike, joshing one another —would ride wagons the five miles to that Bottom farm each spring, dig up foot-long sections of the cane from beds of it that we had covered with dirt against freezing, plant those sections in long rows, and wait. Soon, up would come beautiful new green shoots. As sum-mer streamed along, those shoots shot up higher than a boy's head, then higher than Papa's, and looked like pretty green water pipes two inches or so thick spurting out emerald fountains of fronds in graceful curves. Beautiful! I wish all of you could see a field of young growing sugar cane.

Strip off that soft green outer casing, and lo—inside was the very hard bamboo-like stalk in sections about six to eight or ten inches long. Nature painted it a deep reddish purple and coated that with a strange white powder-like stuff. Strip the hard skin off a section or two, and inside was a softer white fibrous material loaded with lusciousness. There awaited the sap; the juice. It was sheer nectar. You whacked off a little piece with your pocketknife and chewed, then swallowed, and spit out the pulp, and chewed some more, and looked gratefully up to blue heaven and didn't care if you *never* owned a horseless carriage or got to visit Dallas; you had life-luxury enough right here in the cane field.

So, before dawn at a time in autumn, we at home would send down wagonloads of husky men. Papa would accompany on his horse. A benevolent overseer, he would direct the stripping and the cutting, all done by hand at prodigious cost of labor and sweat. Soon the cane would be rows of those stalks standing naked like dark fishing poles. Those fronds would have died back some and started to dry, but the hand labor still was hard.

We had not learned a trick that is used today in the vast cane fields of Hawaii, which Adele and I recently visited. Some years ago, a foreman there had to discharge a worker who was a malcontent and troublemaker. To get revenge, he set fire to the dried, crisp fodder on the standing cane, waiting to be hand stripped. A great holocaust raced through the field. Owners were horrified; the loss of all that cane would be in the hundreds of thousands of dollars because, of course, all the sweet sugar (or syrup) juice in the stalks would be burned or dried out. But when the air cleared and the ash settled, there stood those fat, naked cane stalks, unharmed! The flash fire had simply done the stripping, and at no cost at all. Since then Hawaii has burned off all its cane fodder, at a saving of millions of dollars in labor. It's a shame we didn't discover that trick back in 1905 or so.

Having hand-stripped ours, we then saw big empty wagon beds hauled in. Stripping had been done with great wide-bladed knives, each with a metal hook on the end, a kind of machete. Now the same knife would be swung to clip off the fat stalks near the ground, and the stalks would be tossed into those wagons.

My part in all of that was negligible. Sometimes I might drive one of the wagons, but mostly my much more agreeable duty was to bring "vittles" to the laboring hands. Thus I would leave home in a buggy before eleven A.M. and make my way through Town Square, turn south at the courthouse, and drive down to that Bottom land alongside Town Creek.

Because this was not summer but autumn, my major problem was that old bugaboo called school. I never really liked school anyway, and fortunately, Professor Bittle did not cram it down my throat. In season, he would reason that I might well learn more working with Papa and the Negroes than I would if I pored over an arithmetic book. He was so right! Even now, I am opposed to homework, because it impinges on the process of living and loving and learning in the home; no teacher has a right to claim any child's time after he leaves the campus.

Those heavy loads of cane were mule-hauled about a mile to our surp mill, and soon the beautiful stalks were stacked there like long rows of pulpwood saplings, although the cane stalks were smaller.

The mill itself was on top of a low, flat hill. Huge logs held four perpendicular steel rollers, each about a foot thick and two feet long, all set shoulder high. A boom, made of a stout sapling, extended from the top of those rollers out twenty feet or so. Its upper end was attached to metal cogs in the rollers. Its lower end held a singletree to which was hitched a powerful mule; sometimes two singletrees and two mules. Near the mill was a small stack of those stripped cane stalks, kept replenished by us boys.

"*Heisssst!*" George Austin, our happy foreman and friend, would open the mill work with a between-the-teeth whistle. "Giddap, Blue, you old son of satan."

Good mule Blue would lower his head, dig in, strain mightily, and start the steel rollers turning. George began to poke stalks of cane between the two pairs of them. *SQUISS-S-S-S-SSSH!* How well I remember the sound! How fascinating was the process for us kids and the dozens of guests! The rollers pulled the stalks through and squeezed them virtually dry, and the good juice spurted and ran and dripped down under the rollers where its was caught in a metal basin, then channeled out to one side. There it poured from a lip-like spout and dropped maybe twelve inches into a tow-sack (burlap) strainer stretched over a huge wooden hogshead-type barrel. As the juice came into that strainer, it looked like milk. That's because it became aerated in the squeezing. Later, in the barrel, it would revert to a watery texture and be almost black.

There at the mill, just outside the circle made by Blue's hoofs, were The People. Maybe ten today, maybe forty tomorrow, and thirty the next day; nobody was invited; everybody was welcome. An eagerness shone on them, an expectancy. There, in that initial spurting from the mill, was the most tempting "cold drink" imaginable. Because the autumn mornings were frosty, the stalks were chilled; hence the juice came out colder than any bottled drink we could buy in Town.

Papa, generous host, not only permitted but showed us passel of kids and adults how to get ourselves a bellyfull of that rich, white cane juice. He taken off his big black hat, leaned over, let juice run into his mouth, swallowed prodigiously, stood up, sighed, wiped a mess of white foam off his face, grinned big, and spoke.

"That's how it's done, folks. Step right up. Start with the little ones." He'd point to some three-or-four-year-old. He had already placed a big flat rock near the barrel for them to stand on, but now he would help them reach over the barrel to get the juice.

We drank, and drank, and drank. I have no norm by which I can describe the taste for you. Actually, it was just sugar and water, I think. But Nature may have added some delicate flavorings of her own. I only know that nobody could ever get enough of it. Soon we would start edging out to the bushes—kidneys and bladder can stand just so much—but we would return and drink again. We were harder to satisfy than beer drinkers—which is saying a lot.

Many "guests" of a sort were uninvited. Ten minutes after big George had whistled for Blue to begin, bees arrived. *They* know a good thing when they see it, too; or when they smell it. We had to be wary lest we slurp a live bee into our mouths, or antagonize one and get bayonetted. But we got our revenge by trailing their flight pattern back to bee trees, where the bums were taking our nectar and making their own version of surp. Theirs, I must confess, was much more refined than ours; they had better computerization and mechanization, and packaged theirs much more attractively too. We knew how to raid bee trees and steal large quantities of marvelous honey in the comb. Doing so was a part of this autumn festival each year.

That, then, was the East Texas cane mill.

But didn't the huge barrel eventually get full? So what happened next?

It never got real full. Because at the bottom of it a pipe came out and sloped down that hill about fifty yards to the cooking shed, which I have not heretofore mentioned. But we called all of it a "surp mill," and down there was where the good juice was really converted into surp. Syrup.

Papa presided there over a big flat copper pan about twelve feet long and four feet wide, with sides a foot high. It had dividers, to make three separate sections. All of it had been mounted on a brick structure two feet high, and inside of that we built a log fire. The pipe from the barrel away up yonder extended down to the top of that pan. Papa could twist a spigot and let cold juice run in.

By the time he got his last pan section half full, the first was gently boiling. And We The People, too full of juice to drink any more up yonder with George, stood around the big pan and warmed ourselfs and watched the liquid bubble and plop as Papa gently raked it back and forth with a hoe-like wooden block on a long handle.

As he stirred, the mess in there slowly thickened. Water drifted off in vapor, the residue became ropy and brownish. The sweet aroma became irresistible, but heat kept the bees away. Good, rich, hot cane molasses, syrup, was being made. There is some slight technical difference between "molasses" and "syrup," I do believe, but we used the terms interchangeably; molasses is a cruder but more nourishing product. Papa would sweat from the heat, and talk stuff-and-things with all of us while he worked.

Slightly conscience stricken, the guests all tried to help. Too often, they would only get in the way. They did bring in all the deadwood needed for the fire, ranging into the oak and hickory trees for it, bringing driftwood left after floods. And they did tote hundreds of empty gallon jugs from wagons to cooking pan, lining them up under the big rain shed there. They did hold the funnel when Mr. Will decided the surp was done and ready to draw off. He'd cut down the fire by pulling out blazing logs, then start with the pour-out spigot over funnel and jug at the other end near the chimney.

Meanwhile, us youngsters had broken off the little ends of corncobs, scraped them reasonably free of chaff, and laid them close to hand. They were used to stopper the jugs filled with very hot surp. The matter of sterilization, or even washing, never entered our minds; those cobs had come from our horse and mule feed troughs at home, where the animals had eaten the corn off them. They looked spanking clean. The jugs had been made by Mr. Russell in his wonderful pottery just across the railroad tracks from us at home. He made them by hand, kicking the big lever that turned a flywheel and the mud turntable above. Sometimes he would "let" me sit under there and turn that wheel; *let* me, as the fictional Tom Sawyer "let" his friends help whitewash a fence. We also used some gallon cans with metal press-on tops, but nobody really liked those. They were just cheaper, lighter, and less likely to bust if dropped. But good surp belonged in jugs.

So there we were, maybe thirty of us altogether. A new group was present each of the ten or twelve days required to do up the cane. We came in sensible old clothes with warm outer garments. We gathered for pleasure at the Arnold surp mill, located in a pristine forest where we could see many rabbits, squirrels, birds, and deer if we took time to look around.

For my part, I would show up before noon with my buggy load of grub—dozens of huge buttered biscuits, big cans of hot collard or turnip greens, other cans of chicken-fried steaks or roast beef from a yearling we had butchered, jugs of cold buttermilk. I was a hero upon arrival; people sprang to help me unload and water my horse and hobble him to graze. Nobody had a watch, but our stomachs knew. Anyway, we could hold a hoe handle straight up and study its shadow and know when 12 o'clock came, our primitive but effective version of a sun dial.

"TAKE OFF, GEORGE!" Papa would shout.

George would whoa old Blue and turn him loose to drink water, wallow, and rest, then eat oats brought especially for him. If my buggy horse tried to horn in on those oats, Blue would back his ears and kick the stuffin' out of him. After dinner George would use maybe Jack or Doc or Houston, the latter a great mule named for the founder of Texas. Now the mill would lie still, except for dripping. George would walk to the brook, wash his face and hands with much spluttering against the chill of it, lie on his belly to drink, wipe his face on a huge red bandana, laugh, and likely pick up a little child to put on his shoulder and tote him to dinner near the warmth of the syrup pan. Seeing all of that minutae in memory, my heart once more is warmed. Before I got too biggety, I was the happy child sometimes; but I had to ride piggyback, being already gangly.

As I grew along for a few years, I became the mill man-of-all-service. I must have been about ten to fifteen during that interval, so I could do many things. First, I gave each person one of those metal syrup-can lids. It amounted to a small dinner plate. I drawed off—all right, drew—a tin pitcher of that hot, hot surp from the great pan. I poured some over each biscuit on each plate. I brought each person some beef and greens on another lid. Then we all set cross-legged on dry leaves, and et.

You swiped your biscuit onto your plate of hot surp, took a huge bite, added a blob of steak, and broth-*er*! Your cheeks bulged, and so did your happiness. I'd pass tin cups of the cold buttermilk to wash everything down. We would eat the collard or turnip greens with little forked sticks cut from green limbs nearby. Often we would have "sweet'n-yam" 'taters, baked in the hot ashes.

Mama and Ellen Austin came down there rarely, but enjoyed it when they did. Uncle Johnny was always off somewhere teaching school. Even Grady and Buck were usually off at college, although they got in on some of the surp festivals. Sis was too busy establishing a home after she and Ned Preston were married in 1910, but she would ride her horse—sidesaddle, of course—down there now and again. Sidesaddle, because shapely young women in those years did not show their legs; excuse me—*limbs*. But big brother Tip seems to have been there many times, as I think back.

Often he would have come down early and shot us a mess of squirrels out of the nearby hickory or oak trees, with some little Negro boy turning them for him. The boy would walk around the tree, and Mr. Squirrel up there would see him and go around to the other side of the trunk to hide, and Tip would be on *that* side with a cocked rifle. Sneaky! This game would be dressed out and roasted on spits over the same piles of coals that cooked the cane juice. Tastier than the cow steaks, I vow.

Again, it might be a pile of tender young cottontail meat. More rarely, venison. Often, bobwhites and doves. Tip knew how to work magic with rifle or shotgun. Next day it might be fish. With anybody to help him—and plenty were eager to—he would make a dozen or so swipes in the bigger pools of the creek there, using a fine-mesh seine. Invariably they would lift out a lot of bream, crappie, bass, buffalo, drum, goggle-eyes, even catfish. With so much eager help at hand, it was no problem to scale, skin, and gut them and quick-roast them (three to five minutes; fish must not be dried out when charcoaled) on a stretch of fine-mesh chicken wire. Fun!

I recall that the fish particularly appealed to Mr. Oscar Rogers, the prominent business man in Town who liked to drive down. He also took pleasure in fraternizing with the country people who gathered. Among my own friends, I could bring Lank Wood and Tunk Griffin on Saturdays. That year, when me and Mary-Margaret Sara O'Reilly were planning to be married some day (we were merely urchins at the time) I let her ride down there with me in the grub buggy and I even kissed her once, en route. But the trip didn't work out well because people teased us and we both got hacked. Most of the guests, I suppose, were just "ordinary" folks, who had too little partying of any kind in life, and who truly enjoyed this open-hearted hospitality at the surp mill.

We stored the jugged syrup in a shed built for it there near the cooking pan, but never thought of locking the door. One day Mr. Jimmerson, out hunting squirrels after surping season was over, caught a trampy looking white man stealing some of Papa's filled jugs. With his gun he made the man ride his old rickety wagon right on up to our house and turned him over to Papa to be sent to jail. But the man swore he done it because his wife and kids were hungry and they had next to no food, so Papa gave him a five-dollar bill and told him to keep the syrup too.

Likely by now you can envision at least some of the "atmosphere" at our surp-makin' festivals. I mean, the talk was as good as the cold cane juice and the hot 'lasses and the food. Almost. Joking and joshing and laughing are the main ingredients of any such gathering. For all of us there was a sense of well being; of contentment; peace of mind. There may have been troubles in Austin and Washington (the dad-danged Kaiser was snarling at us) and likely some problems closer to home. If so, we did not nurse them in our minds there in the warmth of the fellowship and of the syrup-pan fire.

The people had sensed their welcome; the common people; the wonderful people. Of course it cost Papa a little money, in cane juice and food and such, but we did not equate hospitality with cash. Come to think of it, what good is money anyway? In our self-sustaining pattern of life, we used or needed very little of it.

I wish you could have been there.

 *Hog-Killing Time*

Another grand festival was recurrent each winter season. It, too, was ritualistic to a degree. It, too, was deeply ingrained in the American folk way. It, too, was vital to our economy, because from it came major items of our food supply. It would be anticipated as early as September, but three more months usually had to pass before events could be tightened down. Christmas would be in the offing, and there would be a definite need then.

By December 1, both Papa and Mama, and Uncle Johnny if he were around, would have been "studyin' " the weather. As many a rural citizen does, they had become expert at it. They had no scientific approach. They did have sundry advance pains in their bones—and just here in 1974 scientists have determined that bodily reactions, pains from rheumatism or arthritis or whatever, *can* be relied on as accurate barometric predictions. The old country folk knew it all the time. They predicted, and without any superstitious mumbo-jumbo. Cold weather was vital to our winter festival.

One typical eight P.M. in my memory, Papa just stood on the back porch near the kitchen door, wet a finger, and held it up. No, not to test the wind, but to sort of feel the atmosphere. He was studying the sky, where a crescent shepherded a flock of stars. I do not know exactly what message he got from that cosmic research; but some long-range instinct, inherited perhaps from Adam himself, told him that the time had come, that tomorrow would be the Day.

"OREN!" he bellowed. Evidently he thought I was in before the fire.

"Sir?" I was right near his coat tail, an eager urchin.

"Ah, boy. Didn't see you. Well, there'll be ice in the morning. Go tell the people."

"Yes, sir!"

No detailed instructions were necessary, I knew what to do. The air was already biting, so I hastily put on my stocking cap—a silly, long, red thing Aunt Nannie had knitted for me, which eternally flopped in my way, but which was fashionable in that period and, I believe, still is for ice-skaters and such. I added a heavy maroon sweater, which I my own self, with my own money, had ordered from a Sears, Roebuck catalog. I put on mittens. I already had on stockings and high-topped work shoes, not my pretty Sunday ones that buttoned down the sides. So I grabbed seven teacakes from the pantry and took off.

It didn't take me hardly no time a-tall to run down the long lane and rush panting along the Negro colony, shouting "HOG KILLIN'!" at the door of each home.

At each one, I heard a hearty scraping of chairs, a sudden clatter of feet and voices. I knew that I had delivered good news, but I didn't wait for discussion, I raced on to the next home. But, at the last house, Donie Murphy had already heard me shouting from two houses away, so she was on her porch, her arms holding herself tight in the chill, smiling, and standing silhouetted against her fireplace glow inside.

"Oren boy, we heard you! We sho glad. But you come on in heah, chile, and wahm yo'self. You boun' to be col'."

I was, in spite of my running. My face burned with it, my nose dripped. I went in, held my hands to the fire, talked with huge Henry, her husband, who was the engine tender down at the depot; also with Foster Murphy, their son, who was my age and my friend. Foster was happily eating a bowl of hot corn mush from a skillet there on the fireplace coals. His mom Donie brought me a bowl and gave me some and poured milk on to cool it, and I sat cross-legged on the hearth with Foster and we both et.

"We gits us a bladduh tomorrow, hunh?" said Foster.

"Natch," said I, buddy-buddy, boy-to-boy. A hog bladder; a big part of the butchering festival, for us.

"And de lights?"

"The lights," I nodded.

"And de nuts?" Foster was slurping his mush eagerly, eyeing me. But his daddy quickly spoke out.

"Naw, suh, boy. You knows who gits dem. Me! and George and Milus and Uncle Handy Grindy and all us men. Mistuh Tip hisself, he crazy 'bout hog nuts. He gonna want some."

We were not disappointed; we had expected that. Adult males could not always be circumvented by small boys. Anyway, we, too, would grow up soon and have first pick. Calmly, we ate on.

"And de gedneys?" Foster continued, undiscouraged, eying me.

I was about to say not likely. But his mama put in.

"Naw you ain't. Us wimmens, we gets de gedneys. Miss Archie always say so."

"Aw," groused Foster.

"Tell you what, tho'. Miss Archie, she mos' likely to give you chilluns some of de lean trimmin's along with yo' lights and bladduhs, and you can cut some green switches and roas' dat good meat over de hot coals where we boils watuh. How 'bout dat?" Donie smiled big. She really loved us children, and we sensed it.

Warmed, fed physically and spiritually, I departed. It had taken me maybe an hour, but I trudged home happy in the star and moon glow, puffing out vapor in the cold. I was shucking my clothes off before our fire when Papa spoke again.

"Better oil your rifle."

"Yes, sir."

"Then get to bed," Mama put in. "We'll all have a busy day."

I took my hot flatiron in its wrapping upstairs to my feather bed, undressed down to my longies, and dived under the four quilts. I knew that at least twenty people besides our family would be in our backyard soon after breakfast. I knew that George Austin would already have a warming fire blazing, and another one under our huge black iron watering pot, brought from the barnlot. I knew that the block and tackle would already be strung up on the strong limb of the elm tree out there, and that a large water barrel would be half buried under the dangling ropes, ready to hold scalding water.

I also knew that such anticipatory thinking was being done by those other people on this evening of stillness and cold. Anticipation is always the best part of life, it seems; no, not always, for some things not only live up to expectations, but exceed them; such as sex, and good food, and visiting the Grand Canyon, and swimming in ocean surf. But in anticipation we can generally enjoy something before it happens, and I did just that in my featherbed. Tomorrow, I told myself, snuggled around my hot iron in the attic room upstairs, would be hog killing time.

Six big waddly grunting animals were to be butchered. We took them one at a time. I can recall, with not too much shame, how I swaggered because I was the designated rifleman. My brother-in-law, Ned Preston, had a .22-calibre repeater and he had taught me to be expert with it. Together, in fun, we even imitated the gun showmen who came around with the 101 Wild West Show. For instance, it was, and still is, easy to turn your back to a tin can, say, fifty feet away, point the .22 backward over your shoulder, hold a little mirror on the stock and hit that can five times out of five. How that did impress spectators!

But Papa also had a single-shot .32 that carried far more clout, and I knew that if I drilled any hog at a specified spot just behind the ear the bullet would strike the brain and kill him instantly. I shot from close range, and the first heavy animal toppled in its tracks, quivering a little.

Uncle Johnny, home that week, had already honed a dozen butcher knives of assorted shapes and sizes to razor-like sharpness. Now Papa took a long thin one, stooped and stuck it deep into the hog's heart. Blood gushed dramatically. It was a good opener, a mind catcher for the festival.

Bled, my slain hog next was hitched to a singletree, the metal hooks stuck through flesh so as to link with heel tendons, which were exceedingly strong. A harnessed mule dragged it to that half-buried barrel, into which guests had already poured many gallons of boiling water.

Now the singletree was unhitched from the mule and tied to the block-and-tackle rope dangling overhead. Half a dozen eager hands grabbed the long rope. Pulley wheels shrieked a protest over somebody's having failed to oil them, and Papa looked hard at me. It had been my duty. Up went the carcass, dangling head down, and guided to a point right over the barrel. The rope men slacked off so that the carcass eased into the water, with a great hissing and bubbling of white vapor that we miscalled steam (real steam is invisible). Meanwhile almost everyone was talking and laughing and giving unnecessary instructions, but Papa designated four men to take wide-bladed butcher knives and stand ready. Only a minute or so in that hot water was required. The hog was pulled up and out, then swung aside and tied, still dangling. The four men moved right in and began scraping. Hot water had loosened hair as it loosens feathers on a scalded chicken. In barely five minutes, there hung an extremely fat, white treasure, and Papa said, "All right, George."

With deft strokes of his knife, George slit the hog straight down the belly and out dropped the guts into a big zinc washtub. Right away me and Foster Murphy and some other little niggers got the lights—lungs—so at once we put these on long green sticks to roast for eating, with only a little salt to season. We waited patiently for the bladder, and presently George tossed it to us.

It was huge, because the hog was. Foster took it, drained out all the urine, squzz—squeezed—it and put the three-inch nipple, or drainage canal, into his mouth. His cheeks bulged and he blowed. That rubbery bladder became a ten-inch globe, so we tied the nipple and, with other kids, ran aside to launch a game of football. Great! Let the renowned Texas Longhorns, Oklahoma Sooners, USC Trojans, Notre Dame Irish, and their ilk have all the Cotton Bowls, Rose Bowls, and Sugar Bowls they want, in their stark professionalism under the guise of college youth in amateur play. We had the most fun, and without self-delusion or subterfuge.

By noon, big three-inch-thick slabs of fat had been cut up and were boiling in a pot to make lard. When it was done, Negro women drained off the grease and put the meat cuts on a table to cool. Half an hour later—hard, brown cracklin's! Delicious! Everybody ate of them, again with only a bit of salt. The clear liquid grease was poured into tall crocks, where it would harden into snowy white lard. Recently I was having dinner as a guest of friends in a super-deluxe club on top of a skyscraper in a great city. The lavish buffet table had "marble" sculptures up to two feet high that would do justice to Michelangelo, and I asked the chef what material he had used. Said he, "Lard." I wish we had thought about sculpturing hard lard back there in olden Texas; we could have had us a lot of fun.

While our lard was cooking, tubs full of lean trimmings were being stuffed into the maw of a grinding mill, along with the sage, salt, pepper, and assorted "yarbs"—herbs—which only Mama knew about, and with which the trimmings had been marinated. We bigger kids took turns at that mill, for a while, revolving the big handle. But we soon tired and ducked out, and Uncle Handy took over, as he had done annually for years.

Uncle Handy was close to a century old. He had been a slave, as had some of his children. Now he was an ageless old hunk of charcoal with no teeth, almost no eyesight, no kinfolk, no future, no money, no responsibilities. Papa "kept" him, assisted by good-natured Negroes who gave him a warm place to sleep. He never lacked for anything essential, never needed a doctor. One day he just up and died from sheer old age. As a black baby of unknown parentage, he had never acquired a name. But because he was "handy" at many little jobs around a farm, and especially because he was somewhat the center of attention at hog killing time, when he turned the sausage grinder, he acquired the surname Grindy.

Names of people have always fascinated me, and his was no exception. I submit that a man can go to heaven named Handy Grindy as quickly and happily as one named Francisco Delgado Mariones Juan del Tafoya de la Cota y Bustamente, who is a Mexican gentleman I know in Arizona. Once, too, I knew a man named Kip Zip. Our Handy was called "Uncle" out of affection, as were many other oldsters, both black and white. Once, when a sassy neighbor kid was caught trying to tease and ridicule Uncle Handy, my Papa grabbed the urchin and spanked him. "He is just young," Uncle Handy said. Papa replied, "He is older now than he was a moment ago." Handy Grindy was loved. Millions of men cannot carry that fact with them when they face Saint Peter beseeching entrance.

Uncle Handy loved bacon—raw. Never mind any possible trichinosis; we had never heard of any disease latent in hog meat. So he would help trim the slabs of fresh side meat, which would be hung in the smokehouse to age and cure, along with the shoulders and hams. Continually, he sucked on bits of the fresh fat.

Today, too, the hog's head had to be prepared; the backbone, with its delicious gnawing meat, had to be cut into convenient lengths, the sparerib sections whacked with a cleaver, folded and made ready for use. Then there were the feet, with their delicious gelatinous "knuckles," and the head with endless tidbits. The stomach was made ready for tripe—have you delicate dudes ever et tripe? Don't cringe; you could do worse. But not much, I admit. All day the routine went on, until six big porkers had been processed.

Three or four times, on freezing morns after Christmas, the butchering would be repeated. Several of the same people would be there, but new ones would show up, too; often some we didn't even know. That made no difference. Papa would just walk to them, extend a hand and say, "Will Arnold." Rigid social protocol required the stranger to say, "Pleased to meetcha," then add his own name. Even children had to say that, if they weren't too shy. Also, the adult stranger would invariably add, "Like to help any way I can, Mr. Will." That too was requisite, and Papa would nod acknowledgment. If there was a woman stranger, Papa would bring Mama up and say, "This here's my wife Archie," and the pleased-to-meetcha ritual would be heard again. Formality, with sparks and smoke from the water-boiling and warming fires drifting around them, joining warm breath vapor in the cold air. It makes a picture I do not forget.

The most memorable guest, ever, was a rather swarthy white man about thirty-five years of age with a coal-black moustache thi-i-i-is long, the tips of it almost touching his ears. He was unforgettably handsome; ask my sister Opal or, forsooth, my pal Bonny Flanagan. He had on red pants—red! Today in the 1970's I, too, have red pants, and think nothing of it. But back there——! Tucked into them was a silken yellow shirt, tight at the cuffs but very full and flouncy in the sleeves. He wore shiny boots and a patent leather cap. I saw the neck of a blue turtle-neck sweater behind the open collar, against this day's cold. But best of all, he carried a fiddle.

Instantly I knowed who he was. Oh, not by name. But last week three wagons of Gypsies had encountered Papa on the dirt road back of our farm and asked permission to camp a few nights beside one of

our springs. You know full well what Papa said. He also asked if they had food, and they confessed to being short, so he decided to give them a calf to butcher. But believe it or not, Gypsies preferred never to kill any animal, even for food, although they will avidly gather the meat of any that has died a natural death. So next day Papa saw to it that the bull calf died naturally—he just naturally clouted it in the forehead with a sledge, put the carcass in a hack and drove it to the Gypsy camp. "It was dead in a rocky ditch," said he, "right where it had fell." That was the literal truth, of course. They accepted the gift.

Now here the picture-book man was, him and his fiddle, settin' on an upended hunk of oak log near our hog-killing fires. The work went slowly that day; everybody was too prone to stop, look, and listen. He spoke almost no English, but he spoke Esperanto, or equal, with his violin. His tunes, foreign to us, nevertheless came out hauntingly beautiful. Some seemed to wail of tragic events, in wild discordant minor keys; others spoke of lilting birdsong and of maidens tripping around Maypoles. My guess now is that he had come from Hungary. But from our culture, he smilingly learnt hisself a new hog killin' tune, right there. While he had rested briefly, George Austin unconsciously broke into his beloved *The little Lord Jesus say to me, Come set heah under this big tree,* while busily slicing meat. When he paused to get more meat, the violin echoed that Dixieland folk tune.

"I be dogged!" murmured George, pausing, smiling big.

"Aw-w-w-w-w." murmured Mama, "how sweet!"

She was right.

We didn't get as much done that day as we usually did, but who cared. A romantic stranger had come to say thank you to Papa in his very special way. We had all *lived.* Gypsies fascinated me then, and still do. Given opportunity, I might join them right now.

 *Rocking-Chair Court*

Inevitably, the time came when William Daniel Arnold and Archibald Laetitia Barry Arnold began to get along. It happens to most of us. One day you feel sixteen but you are sixty-five, and it's ridiculous. Those two old children of the South had been born with a life expectancy of no more than forty years, which was the average for babies of the Civil War era. So, psychologically, they felt "old" when all their five surviving children had left the big white house on the hill.

Then one day some fellow offered Papa twelve thousand dollars for his home and acreage, an excellent price. Shrewd Ned Preston said, "Dad, you better take it. There is a small house right near Doll and me down town. We can buy it for a song, and you and Mother will be right close there where we can look after you."

Papa didn't want no looking after; he had always been self-reliant to a fault. Profane old Cousin Give-a-damn Jim Holloway, a cherished if eccentric relative, often said that Will Arnold was too inde-goddamnpendent. He spoke a crumb of truth there.

But age is immutable, so with Mama's permission Papa up and sold out. Firm-jawed his way through the traumatic experience of getting rid of both big farms, all the stock, all the equipment, most of the furniture, and moving into that rather small cottage just spittin' distance from daughter Opal's home. Mama and Sis could holler-gossip with one another from back porch steps.

Everybody said how nice it was. But, at once, Papa began going to seed. He began letting himself stoop some, and neglecting to shave, looking glassy-eyed, forgetting too many things. He brought a rocking chair out of the house, set it under a great sycamore tree on their side lawn, put a heavy hair-out sheepskin on it, and settled his weary old bones in that nest to live out his final years. He was done. Through. Licked. Finished. His voice developed a rather weak, self-pitying tremolo, where for many years it had boomed. Gnarled old hands shook a little; the same hands that for decades had been so expressive, so dependable, so strong. His back hurt, and the rheumatiz grew worse in his leg. All this in just a few days.

Mama was more sensible. She went happily about establishing a new routine in her smaller, more convenient town home. It had good electric lights; even a water toilet—wasn't that wonderful? George and Ellen Austin had died—and may God never forget such good friends—but Archie neither needed nor wanted help now anyway. But poor Will. He just sat out there, moping, staring off. Opal and Ned worried, fearful that he might soon just die there.

"Fiddle," said Mama when they mentioned it, and went on planting her new little plot of turnip greens. The Will Arnolds of earth were never prone to die, she allowed.

For nine straight days Will sat out there in boredom and near silence, peeking neighbors said. Only a few friends stopped by; most figured he needed rest.

But at about ten o'clock of the tenth day of his retirement, he suddenly stood up, kicked that rocking chair hard against the wall of the house, stalked the five blocks down to Town Square—and, for cash, bought himself a grocery store!

Now, friends and fellow citizens, my Papa knew almost as much about running a grocery store as he knew about space travel to Mars. That fact did not deter him at all. It was as if old Uncle Doc Dawson had shot him with a hypodermic of adrenalin. What's a mere sixty-five years? I have heard tell, allowed he, of men who lived past ninety. And borned children to boot. Wasn't there something like that even in the Bible? Uncle Johnny said yes, there was, but that he better not try acting coltish.

His grocery was on North Marshall street not more than half a block from the venerable Mays and Harris mercantile store. This meant that it was right in the heart of things. The post office was just yonder a few steps. So was the Southwestern Hotel, where drummers gathered. A hundred yards north and you'd come to the cotton yard, which in spring was the grounds for a big Chatauqua tent, followed by a marvelous carnival. Papa had loved the carnival all those years, even if Chatauqua lectures sort of left him cold. Him and me, we saw eye to eye about that, in my youth. The carnival had mo-o-o-ore grand things! A flyin' jenny, a ferrious wheel, four theaters in which might-nigh half-nekkid girls sang and danced and winked at us boys who had paid a quarter to get in, a hundred-foot high-dive ladder, from the tip-top of which a man dove into a net each midnight, a bearded lady you could see for a dime, a place to throw baseballs at bottles on a shelf, heavens I don't know what all! And Papa loved the carnival no less than I. Now his grocery was in a prime location.

But the store itself was close to zero. Its previous owner had displayed negligible merchandising acumen and the place was sadly run down. Apparently it had not even been swept out in months, but Papa paid my old friend Foster Murphy a dollar to clean it good. However, Foster could do nothing about the general shabbiness, the lack of paint and polish, the rusted fly screens, the scuffed floor, the showcases dating back to 1890, the poor lighting, or the fly-specked ceiling with its warped boards.

Even worse was the merchandise. Some of the canned goods had been resting and rusting there for years. A big box of dried apples had worms in it, and two barrels of flour were speckled with weevils. Plug tobacco was too old and hard to chew. Half a big round of cheese on its covered table under its slicing knife had virtually turned to rock, but Papa gave that to a little Negro boy who happened along and the lad seemed delighted. Papa beheld all this mess seemingly undisturbed.

Immediately, though, he had somebody haul a tremendous icebox to the store and set it before the front window on the broad sidewalk. I well remember that box. It was at least six feet long, four wide, and three deep. The lid was so thick and heavy that Papa devised a pulley and weight to help hinge it up. Every other day Marvin Cain, the town iceman, would stop his wagon at the curb and, with great steel tongs, shoulder in a hundred-pound block. The drip from it just peedled on the sidewalk as a puppy might, then ran on across the walk and into the street, where dogs lapped it now and again. Every other day Mr. Culp's bottling-plant wagon would stop there, and the driver would unload four cases of soda pop, mostly red. Papa and Foster would put the twenty-four bottles from each case into the box close to that block of ice.

Having finished all that hard labor before ten of a typical morning, Mr. Will then decided he had done his duty for the day, so he sat down in his rocking chair there beside the icebox. He had carried that same rocker the five blocks from his home lawn to his store, where it sat on the sidewalk night and day. Very soon, he was occupying it with all the dignity of a king on his throne.

There the New Will Arnold, the rejuvenated old farmer and rancher, held court.

He stopped everybody who came by, just to visit. Most people were pleased to bide a wee. They would sit on upended pop cases and talk of everything from the state of affairs between the United States and Germany to the state of affairs between Miss Minerva Traylor, the old maid, and Mr. Gladfelter, who was courting her. But Mr. Glad had *been* courting her since about 1900, so that topic was not a very live one.

Often as many as a dozen men and boys would be gathered there, some of them black, some white, all friendly and prone to whittling and joshing and chewing and expectorating. Each new arrival, right on up to dark at night, and even later if desired, could feel free to get a bottle of pop from that icebox. No charge was made. The pop cost only fifty cents a case, and the ice didn't cost much. It all made good advertising, Papa rationalized. But nobody ever saw any of those loafers and friends make a purchase inside.

Let's say a customer did appear. Like maybe "Miss Addie" Welch, Fate Welch's fine wife. I saw her come once, typically.

"Mornin, Will," she beamed her greeting. "How are you?"

Papa got to his old feet. He would have died right there rather than not show full courtesy to any female. "Fine, Addie, just fine. Tickled to see you, honey. Set and have a pop. Strawberry?"

"Don't mind if I do. How's Archie?"

"More than tollable. Fact is, she's frisky. But mad at me for buyin' this store." He chuckled, and everyone else laughed.

"Can't say as I blame her, Will. You'll work your fool self to death."

Not likely. But he cherished the concern anyway. He gave her the pop after carefully wiping the mouth of it to shiny cleanliness with the palm of his dirty old hand. She did not notice. She sat and swigged it down, sighing gratefully on that warm morning, and said she wondered if there was any extract of vanilla in the store.

"Why, I don't misdoubt but what there is, Addie. You just go on in there and make yourself at home. Look around. *Ought* to be some, I vow."

There was some. Four dozen bottles that some drummer had arbitrarily sent him. He'd likely sell five or six a year.

Drummers did take advantage of his carelessness, by overstocking him with nearly everything they sold. He simply allowed them to go inside alone, poke around, and order what they felt he needed or would pay for. You can imagine their lack of restraint, they being city-dude slickers from Dallas or Houston, or somewhere, anyway. Drummers never did rate very high with us Henderson people; they were too prone to make sly remarks at and about our town girls. But Papa didn't know that; only us young sophisticates were hep.

Almost no customer paid cash. "Keep track of it for me, Mr. Will," they would say, totin' off a big arm load of stuff. He might not even know what all they had.

So maybe he would or maybe he wouldn't "keep track" of it. If his attention wasn't diverted, he might pencil a crude entry in a tiny black book kept in his pocket. Sometimes he would tear off a corner of wropping—not wrapping—paper and pencil the charge memo on that. "Sebe Haskins 80¢." No date, no itemization. When big brother Buck came to visit once, he found a bunch of those notes jammed in a box with some spools of O.N.T. sewing thread. But a mama mouse had made herself a nest in there and was suckling a mess of wormy pink babies, so Papa wouldn't let Buck disturb things. Buck got mad and went on back to Houston, but he did return later and *try* to straighten out our merchant-father. Buck sent four collectors around town, and, bless Jesus, if they didn't come back with nearly eleven hundred dollars! Papa was so proud he walked down to the Rusk County News office to tell Colonel Bob Milner, leaving the store unattended most of that whole morning.

Sometimes a housewife would telephone her order to Papa. But he would visit with her, and forget what all she wanted. Even so, he was dutiful. He would gather up a big box full of assorted stuff and have Foster Murphy put it in the Arnold Dodge touring car and deliver it. Likely she got better than she had ordered. Likely she never paid for all of it, either, because no bill accompanied, and she forgot. Few people were intentionally dishonest. They willingly paid when Buck sent those collectors to them. Most were embarrassed at their own negligence. Life in Henderson in those years was just that casual and easy going, and Papa's heart was—well, you know.

One time when I showed up there from college, I went out riding with Papa in that Dodge car. But he kept saying "Giddap" and "Whoa" to it, so I made him let me have the wheel. Right away I felt a malfunctioning, a raspy sound.

"Papa," I asked, "When did you last change the oil in this thing?"

He looked blank and asked, "What oil?"

Nobody had ever told him. I stopped, inspected the crankcase. Dry as a bone. Not one drop! Creeping to the nearest garage with it, I had four quarts put in. Sure enough, no harm had been done; the car ran like a Rolls Royce.

And now, dearly beloveds, I am going to leave matters just there.

That store enriched Papa's "retirement" years, even if it was a financial disaster. The insolvency did not really hurt him, and the fun he had did him immeasurable good. Because, there near the square of his personal hometown, he could constantly be in touch with The People he loved. The *wonderful* people, if I may. The Will Arnold outreach and hospitality never waned. Holding court from his rocker, he was a happy man.

A contemporary of his tagged that for Will Arnold, without actually knowing him at all. He was a preacher in Papa's own Baptist denomination, but in another state. His name was Kerr Boyce Tupper, and he had this to say about facing up to retirement:

You will not grow old by living long, but by the loss of interests, the lowering of ideals and the waning of enthusiasms. If there is in you a growing capacity for sweet wonder, an increasing appreciation of the beauty in the world, a kindling ardor for knowledge, a mounting gratitude for the tender mercies of God, you are surely and steadily growing young. You will be younger next year than you are now. You are as young as your hopes, as old as your fears, as young as your love of love, as old as your will to hate.

Not until your enthusiasms perish can you ever grow old.

We know that Papa at least sensed the truth in all of that. Because, years before, far out into the sweet potato vines, he had thrown the key that would have locked selfishness and fear inside his heart.

A Boundless Privilege, the fifth book produced by Madrona Press, has been printed on Warren's Olde Style white wove, a paper manufactured for long life. Type used for text is eleven-point Garamond with two point leading, set on Intertype by G & S Typesetters, Austin. Printing by offset lithography was done by Capital Printing Company of Austin, binding by Custom Bookbindery of Austin.

Design by William A. Seymour

MADRONA PRESS, INC.
AUSTIN, TEXAS